Praise for *Social Media Tools for Learning*

"Social media is playing a critical role in education. This book is a practical resource that can be very helpful."

—**Gail Pletnick**, AASA president; Arizona Superintendent of the Year; superintendent, Dysart Unified School District

"Kudos to you on a very timely, detailed, and necessary piece of work. I especially liked the chapters on collaboration and legal issues in using social media. This book gave me succinct examples and a roadmap for improving collaboration among all members of my own team. Every manager and educator needs to read this book and take every word to heart."

—**Ken Carpenter**, MD, adjunct professor of medicine, Division of Gastroenterology, Vanderbilt University School of Medicine; staff physician, Tennessee Valley Healthcare System

"This new book is truly leading edge stuff! Comes at the right time, as we all work to engage in new and exciting ways! Dan and Katie are tops when it comes to providing timely information in a compelling way!"

—**Thomas P. Jandris**, PhD, senior vice president and chief innovation office (CINO); dean, College of Innovation & Professional Programs, Concordia University Chicago

"The authors give excellent examples of education technology as well as practical uses of the technology tools with advantages and disadvantages."

—**Pauline M. Sampson**, PhD, dean of Research and Graduate Studies, Stephen F. Austin State University

"Not a millennial? Not sure about which social media are which? Wozniak and Tomal spell out the definitions, advantages, disadvantages, and 'how to use' for each type of social media. This book can be your invaluable tool."

—**D. William Dodds**, EdD, executive director, Illinois ASCD

"Tomal and Wozniak clearly understand the role that social media has in the future of educational technology and learning. This book is a practical resource in understanding the impact social media has on our culture. I highly recommend the book to all educators or to anyone who wants to use social media in the context of student learning."

—**Robert K. Wilhite**, EdD, dean, College of Graduate Studies, Concordia University Chicago

"Social media has enormous potential to positively impact the work of education leaders, however it is critical that we all understand how best to leverage its power in a strategic and thoughtful manner. The topics outlined and discussed in this book should be of interest to all forward thinking leaders."

—**Kristi Sandvik**, EdD, AASA Executive Board; president elect of the Minority Student Achievement Network

"The authors of this book provide the foundational knowledge and understandings necessary to effectively integrate social media and collaboration tools into instruction. This is a well-written, informative book which establishes an important framework through which to view new and exciting technologies."

—**Carol J. Reiseck**, EdD, associate dean and professor of leadership, Concordia University Chicago

"Social media revolutionized the way millennials communicate with each other. It's an integral part of their day-to-day lives and will evolve even further for the generations to come. I highly recommend this book for integrating social media into the education system."

—**Sean Vitale**, partner and founder, VitalTech Solutions, Chicago

"A must-read for anyone working with learners in the twenty-first century! The authors have created a much-needed resource for understanding and using social media tools to engage learners and maximize learning."

—**Pamela Meyer**, PhD, Center to Advance Education for Adults, DePaul University's School for New Learning

"There has never been a better time to add to the understanding of the role of social media in the school setting. Our kids are 'digital natives' and we owe it to them to get up to speed on this important issue. For teachers and leaders, Tomal and Wozniak have written an important and necessary book. I highly recommend it."

—**Jeffrey T. Brierton**, PhD, adjunct professor of educational leadership, Concordia University Chicago

"Tomal and Wozniak provide timely information about the uses of social media and further engage readers to critically analyze the advantages and disadvantages associated with social media. This book is a practical resource and a must-read."

—**Jon Mielke**, EdD, superintendent Lutheran Schools, Indiana District—LCMS

"The role of social media is critical to the future of educational technology and learning and this book is a practical and understandable resource. I highly recommend this book."

—**Lisa Burmeister**, acting director, Academic Technologies, Concordia University Chicago

"Educators who are interested in the usage of social media and collaboration tools will find this book to be particularly useful. In addition to specific overviews of these tools, this book provides beneficial legal implications for their use."

—**John Schnack**, instructional designer, College of Innovation and Professional Programs

"Connected learning, where students, faculty, staff, and leaders in industry and education come together to share materials and learn new skills with a mindset of community, partnership, collaboration, and creation, is key in today's world. This book envisions and provides examples where students, faculty, and the community come together based on a shared interest to challenge their thinking, learn through action, and produce knowledge using tools such as podcasts, videos, social media, and web-conferencing."

—**Michael J. Sukowski**, acting executive director, Office of Online Instruction and Instructional Technology, Chicago State University

"This much-needed resource provides learning professionals in both K–16 and training and development with a well-balanced guide on how to avoid the pitfalls and make the most of social media for learning."

—**Michelle Navarre Cleary**, PhD, associate professor, DePaul University's School for New Learning

"Dr. Wozniak and Dr. Tomal's research on social media in the classroom is outstanding and at the fore of the field. As the role of social media is increasingly necessary to the future of educational technology and learning, this book is a practical and understandable resource. I highly recommend this book."

—**Christopher J. Lilly**, PhD, chair, Department of Educational Technology, Concordia University Chicago

"This book will get the reader thinking and evaluating their own perspectives on social learning and provides examples of ways to leverage and manage the use of popular social media and collaboration tools to provide engaging teaching and learning opportunities."

—**Ken Sadowski**, SLATE Group

"Social media tools have changed the landscape of learning and connecting in the twenty-first century. The authors have truly captured the 'essence of social media education' in a way that is well written and insightful. I highly recommend this book as a must-read for leaders."

—**Donald F. Gately**, EdD, NYS Principal of the Year 2016; cofounder, EdCamp Long Island; moderator, #NYEdChat Bi-Weekly Twitter Chat for New York State Educators

"This book offers a sound foundation for anyone who studies and uses social media. In the fast lane of social media, knowing the 'why' along with the 'how to' is invaluable."

—**Catherine Marienau**, PhD, professor and coordinator of the MA in Educating Adults, DePaul University

"A great guide for bringing social media into the classroom, and for sending resourceful leaders who communicate effectively through social media out into the world."

—**Steffanie Triller Fry**, MFA, Purdue University Northwest Faculty

"A timely, easy to read, and a practical book on the ins-and-outs of social media. *Social Media Tools for Learning* is a valuable resource that should be on the shelf of all who use the internet."

—**Charles J. Russo**, JD, EdD, Panzer Chair in Education, research professor of law, University of Dayton

"The role of social media is constantly changing. Having the tools to manage social media is critical to any organization. This book is a practical and understandable resource for educators."

—**Craig A. Schilling**, PhD, CEO, Global Workforce Essentials LLC

"This book gets to the basics of social media and can be an excellent resource for explaining the role of social media in education and beyond."

—**Craig Lusthoff**, associate dean, College of Business, Concordia University Chicago

"This book functions not only as a solid pedagogical guide for incorporating social media into the classroom, but also as an accessible resource on the vast array of technologies and theories vital to making this incorporation a success."

—**Shannon Milligan**, PhD, Institutional Research and Market Analytics, DePaul University

"Insightful, detailed, well researched, a much needed academic resource for educational leaders in the new digital age. Will definitely promote new research. If you select one social media publication this year, it should be this one."

—**Michael J. Harkins**, president, Illinois AAUP Conference

"The role of social media is critical to the future of educational technology and learning. This book is a practical and understandable resource—a required reading for all leaders. I highly recommend this book."

—**Sandra C. Coyner**, EdD, professor, The University of Akron LeBron James Family Foundation College of Education

"I recommend this book to all educators who understand the importance of using social media for student learning. Outstanding!"

—Dr. **Claudia Santin**, PhD, dean, College of Business, Concordia University Chicago

"*Social Media Tools for Learning* is an invaluable addition to the expanding narrative supporting the importance of social media use for communicating and sharing ideas locally and globally. The learning landscape in the current century is significantly different than the learning landscape of last century; *Social Media Tools for Learning* will prove to be an effective guide to navigating this change and develop a deeper understanding of how to effectively utilize social media and other tech tools to expand and amplify learning."

—**Art Fessler**, EdD, superintendent of schools

"A timely book. The authors provide an excellent basis for understanding social media. A great practical source for educators."

—**Maja Miskovic**, PhD, executive director for the Division of Research & Doctoral Programs, Concordia University Chicago

"Social media can play a critical role in the educational process, and this book provides the necessary foundation to implement these tools in a way that supports successful learning."

—**Sarah Brown**, assistant director of Faculty Development and Instructional Technology, DePaul University

"The authors have provided a comprehensive yet accessible resource for understanding the use, history, and impact of social media. It is a valuable addition to any social learning curriculum."

—**Kamilah Cummings**, MA, DePaul University School for New Learning Faculty

"The authors succinctly provide an excellent basic for understanding social media. I am more than confident that this book will make a positive contribution in the field of education. This book is definitely an excellent resource for all educators. Job well done!"

—**Beverly A. Hives**, PhD, educator, Cleveland, Ohio

"Social media can be a blessing or a curse in public school education. The authors of this book have provided practical ways for educators to effectively use its capabilities and popularity to leverage positive change in how we communicate and collaborate in the workplace, classroom, and school community."

—**Theron J. Schutte**, PhD, AASA Executive Board, superintendent, Marshalltown Community School District

Social Media Tools
for Learning

Concordia University Chicago Leadership Series
An Educational Series from Rowman & Littlefield Education

Series Editor: Daniel R. Tomal, PhD

Education leaders have many titles and positions in American schools today: professors, K–12 teachers, district and building administrators, teacher coaches, teacher evaluators, directors, coordinators, staff specialists, etc. More than ever, educators need practical and proven educational and leadership resources to stay current and advance the learning of students.

The Concordia University Chicago Leadership Series is a unique resource that addresses this need. The authors of this series are award-winning authors and scholars who are both passionate theorists and practitioners of this valuable collection of works. They give realistic and real-life examples and strategies to help all educators inspire and make a difference in school improvement and student learning that get results.

This Leadership Series consists of a variety of distinctive books on subjects of school change, research, completing advanced degrees, school administration, leadership and motivation, business finance and resources, human resource management, challenging students to learn, action research for practitioners, the teacher as a coach, school law and policies, ethics, and many other topics that are critical to modern educators in meeting the emerging and diverse students of today. These books also align with current federal, state, and various association accreditation standards and elements.

Staying current and building the future require the knowledge and strategies presented in these books. The Leadership Series originator, Daniel R. Tomal, PhD, an award-winning author who has published over 20 books and 200 articles and studies, is a highly sought-after speaker and educational researcher. He, along with his coauthors, provides a wealth of educational experience and proven strategies that can help all educators aspire to be the best they can be in meeting the demands of modern educational leadership.

Social Media Tools for Learning

Activating Collaboration Strategies for Success

Kathryn Wozniak and Daniel R. Tomal

ROWMAN & LITTLEFIELD
Lanham • Boulder • New York • London

Published by Rowman & Littlefield
An imprint of The Rowman & Littlefield Publishing Group, Inc.
4501 Forbes Boulevard, Suite 200, Lanham, Maryland 20706
www.rowman.com

Unit A, Whitacre Mews, 26–34 Stannary Street, London SE11 4AB

Copyright © 2018 by Kathryn Wozniak and Daniel R. Tomal

All rights reserved. No part of this book may be reproduced in any form or by any electronic or mechanical means, including information storage and retrieval systems, without written permission from the publisher, except by a reviewer who may quote passages in a review.

British Library Cataloguing in Publication Information Available

Library of Congress Cataloging-in-Publication Data Available

ISBN: 978-1-4758-3962-3 (cloth : alk. paper)
ISBN: 978-1-4758-3963-0 (pbk. : alk. paper)
ISBN: 978-1-4758-3964-7 (electronic)

Other Books by Kathryn Wozniak and Daniel R. Tomal

Human Resource Management
Songwriting: Strategies for Musical Self-Expression and Creativity
Leading with Resolve and Mastery
Ethics and Politics in School Leadership
Grant Writing: Strategies for Scholars and Professionals
Supervision and Evaluation for Learning and Growth
The Teacher Leader: Core Competencies and Strategies for Effective Leadership
How to Finish and Defend Your Dissertation: Strategies to Complete the Professional Practice Doctorate
Leading School Change: Maximizing Resources for School Improvement
Managing Human Resources and Collective Bargaining
Resource Management for School Administrators: Optimizing Fiscal, Facility, and Human Resources
Action Research for Educators, Second Edition
Challenging Students to Learn: How to Use Effective Leadership and Motivation Tactics
Action Research for Educators
Discipline by Negotiation: Methods for Managing Student Behavior

Contents

Foreword		xiv
Additional Foreword		xvi
Acknowledgments		xviii
	Introduction	1
1	Social Learning in a Digital Age	5
2	Social Learning Theories and Models	21
3	Social Media Tools and Learning	35
4	Collaboration Tools and Learning	56
5	Legal Issues Impacting Social Media	75
6	Evaluation and Moving Forward	93
Appendix A. Common Social Media and Technology Resources		107
Appendix B. Social Media and Technology Trademarks		109
Appendix C. Create Accessible Video and Social Media		111
Appendix D. Electronic Code of Federal Regulations		113
Appendix E. ELCC Building and District Level Standards		114
Appendix F. Technology Standards for School Administrators		122
Index		125
About the Authors		127

Foreword

I know it's a bit of a cliché but, since I started in social media marketing in 2006, times really have changed! Back then, social media was called New Media, and MySpace was the popular site that most people used. When Facebook executives opened Facebook up to the general public after it made a huge impact on the college market, parents and children alike jumped in and opened accounts.

I was so intrigued by social media that I wrote a book, *Everything You Ever Wanted to Know about Social Media, But Were Afraid to Ask: Building Your Business Using Consumer Generated Media*. I also formed an organization, Social Media Association, and at that time, there weren't too many of us, but we would meet at a local diner to discuss blogs and social media marketing. Most importantly, I developed a New Media department at my public relations agency, HJMT Public Relations, Inc.

Little did we all know or think about the implications of data mining and privacy, but we were excited that there was something new to embrace. Most of us were happy to reconnect with old friends and acquaintances on Facebook. When the parents were all on Facebook, the millennials left and joined Snapchat, which was followed by Instagram. Now, Instagram is one of the most important sites, and marketers are focusing on influencers. If these influencers don't have a significant following or engagement on Instagram, then they won't be used to market products and services.

YouTube is still hot, and most millennials and those younger watch YouTube more than they watch television! Twitter has been important and made a recent resurgence since our fellow citizens have been very interested in what the president is doing on a daily basis. Blogs were and will be something that will stick around for a while. There are hundreds of thousands of blogs on a variety of platforms that offer personal experiences to readers.

My first blog, NYLifestyleBlog.com, was formed in 2008, and today has more than 88,000 unique visitors. A few years later, after I started to get athletic in my "older years," I began ATriathletesDiary.com blog and around the same time started a radio podcast, Hilary Topper on Air, which has more than 250,000 listeners. I created my own media "empire," and I'm not alone. There are hundreds of thousands of "influencers" who have a unique following too. This is one of the ways in which social media has become much bigger than we will ever know.

I've been teaching as an adjunct professor, Digital Communications, at Hofstra for their master's program for several years now and have noticed that students bring their mobile devices into the classroom. Many professors won't tolerate this type of behavior, but for me, it not only keeps me on my toes and keeps me current, but I use that to enhance the experience for them. If I say something that's intriguing, I notice that they go on their phones to look up what I'm talking about, then often add to the discussion.

Social media is going to continue to evolve. Books written about the subject will continuously be outdated, and people, even though their data is being mined, will continue to research and enjoy the camaraderie of social media. Special thanks to both Daniel R. Tomal and Kathryn Wozniak for including me in the foreword. This is an important book and I know you will have tons of beneficial take-aways from it!

Hilary J. M. Topper, MPA
President & CEO, HJMT Public Relations, Inc.

Additional Foreword

School district branding, marketing, learning, and showcasing student achievement has become a definitive need for all school districts. While the field of education is a publicly funded arena, school districts are responsible for building their brand and promoting their positive achievements. This is done through a variety of social media platforms such as Facebook, Twitter, Instagram, Snapchat, to name a few. In addition, the integration of the technology standards to utilize these social media platforms for student learning is another use that is gaining momentum in classrooms at all levels of education from higher education to K–12 schools.

The need for a comprehensive book on social media to help school educators address this topic is essential. This book by Kathryn Wozniak and Daniel R. Tomal provides educators with the tools necessary to successfully apply the use of social media in all levels of education and will equip them with the necessary resources for success. As a superintendent of schools, and a proponent of social media, I believe this book covers the critical areas of collaborative learning, tools, technology, legalities, theories and models, and learning in the digital age that are so important for learning today and in the future.

This book is organized in a thoughtful and well-constructed manner. The foundation for social media is presented with research-based theories and models on collaboration learning for both live and online learning environments. The practical strategies for implementing collaborative tools for instruction are thoroughly covered and addressed so that any educator can understand and apply them. The important topic of legal issues in social media provides the essential framework to assist all educators—professors, school district administrators, and K–12 teachers and staff—in applying social media instructional and institutional programs.

I commend the authors for developing this comprehensive and a much-needed book on social media. I am confident the book will be a valuable resource for all educators.

Dr. Bill Robertson
Superintendent of Schools
Fremont School District 79

Acknowledgments

My sincerest gratitude goes to my coauthor, Dan Tomal, for his guidance, inspiration, and patience. This was an invaluable opportunity, and I am grateful our paths crossed.

Much gratitude to the members of the Educational Technology Department and Instructional Design Team at CUC for sharing their time, energy, friendship, and suggestions throughout the process: Chris Lilly, Aaron Kessler, Sam Kwon, Ardelle Pate, Richard Richter, Helga Hambrock, John Schnack, Lisa Burmeister, and Paul Brooner. Thank you also to Jacob Hagan, Don Hendricks, Tony, Annette, James, and all the student workers at the office for helping me to keep a smile on my face.

A special thanks goes to Dean Tom Jandris and Assistant Dean Carol Reiseck for their ongoing intellectual and financial support through the College of Innovation and Professional Programs at CUC. Thank you also to all those who participated in this research and all the lifelong learners out there. You are the driving force behind my passion for learning, teaching, and designing.

Last, but certainly not least, for their unconditional love and support in this and every endeavor I take on, all my love goes to my family and friends including Jake, Mom, Dad, Grandma, Chris, Jenny, Joy, Nancy, Frank, Liz, Carole, Ron, Marilyn, Ann, Karl, Becca, Liz, Pete, Delilah, Nick, Kelly, Richard, Kim, Jason, Lauren, Chrissy, Sarah, Ciara, Erin, Deana, Katie, Cecilia, Mike, Ashleigh, Irene, Carrie, Becca, Yolanda, Vicky, Stefania, Danielle, Shelby, Barb, Tugce, Malena, Tasha, Derek, Jeff, Evie, Sarah, Shannon, Jen, Michelle, Steffanie, Kamilah, Gretchen, Catherine, and Pamela.

Introduction

The use of social media in school districts, higher education, and organizations continues to grow across the country. School branding, marketing, and showcasing student achievement are becoming definitive needs for all school districts. While the field of education is a publicly funded arena, school districts and learning organizations are responsible for building their brand and promoting their positive achievements.

There are myriad social media platforms, such as Facebook, Twitter, Instagram, and Snapchat, to name a few. In addition, the integration of the technology standards to utilize these social media platforms for student learning is another use that is gaining momentum in classrooms. Many school districts, learning organizations, and university educators are also using some form of social media and technology to enhance their teaching. While this may be the case, many educators continue to struggle to understand, maintain, and integrate the use of social media and supporting technology to its fullest capacity.

This book provides a foundation for establishing a social media program in the education institution and how to use social media for school district branding, marketing, and showcasing student achievement. This is a proven model that has been successful in the private sector and is making its way into the field of education. Providing educators and corporate learning leaders with the tools necessary to successfully apply the use of social media in the field of education will equip them with the resources necessary to begin.

While this book is primarily designed for K–12 school districts, it is also very useful for all educators, including those in university settings, and those serving as private and charter school systems, and learning organizations. This information can help all educators improve their understanding of social media and supporting technology concepts that enable the proficient use of social media programs and software, and related computer network supports.

It will also provide practical strategies to help all educators improve their understanding of foundational pedagogical concepts that can be the underpinnings for best practices for designing and using social media to support traditional classroom and online learning.

Specific questions often asked by educators such as those that follow are addressed: What is social media? What are common social media programs? What technology is needed to support a social media program within the school district? How can educators ensure proper and safe use of social media to protect both students and the school district? What are the key issues related to computer security when using social media? What are the best strategies to use social media to support teaching and learning?

Chapter 1 begins by providing an introduction to social media in the digital age. The chapter covers several components of social learning theories such as cognitive, behavioral, and motivation. Several steps are provided that will aid educators and instructional designers in preparing for social learning, such as establishing learning objectives. There is also an exercise to help apply the concepts to education and learning. Additional discussion questions are provided with a list of relevant references.

Chapter 2 presents the fundamentals of social learning theories and terminology. Having a good understanding of learning theories of constructivism and constructionism can be beneficial to an educator in teaching social media. Topics in this chapter include understanding social media, components, significance of social learning frameworks, legitimate peripheral participation, and cognitive apprenticeship. Actual illustrations are presented and explained so that you can understand the basic theories of social media. Several practical examples are also given at the end of the chapter along with discussion exercises and references.

Chapter 3 deals with understanding definitions of social media, distinguishing between various social media features and interactions and benefits, strategies to leverage social media tools, and features to facilitate learning and support learners. The chapter also includes methods to synthesize social learning theory and strategies for using social media tools for learning, and implanting social media technology in teaching. Like the other chapters, this chapter provides a summary of the content, discussion questions, activities, and references at the end of the chapter.

Chapter 4 covers social media collaboration tools, and how to distinguish between various collaborative tools, evaluation and learning strategies, and developing robust learning experiences. Also, perspectives on collaboration tools for learning and strategies for planning and designing collaborative learning activities for online learning are covered. The chapter also includes a relevant case study and questions and exercises.

Chapter 5 covers the topic of legal issues impacting social media. Topics include understanding legal issues; major employment laws associated with social media and learning; and implications of laws and legal issues impacting the conduct of employees, teachers, and students. The important legal characteristics that define a social media are explained. A case study along with exercises and discussion questions are provided to give the reader practice in applying the content of this chapter.

Chapter 6 focuses on evaluation of learning that incorporates social media. An overview of evaluation methods and a research study about the use of social media for learning is included. Results from a social media research study are presented along with several comments from social media educators. The chapter concludes with exercises where the reader can apply his or her understanding of social media.

FEATURES OF THE BOOK

This book is succinctly written and an easy read for graduate students, practicing teachers, technology professionals, school administrators, and university professors. This book is unique in that it provides many engaging examples that can help educators understand basic social media terminology, technology devices, troubleshooting, operations, and social media–enhanced instruction. Each chapter's objectives are aligned with professional organizational standards of the *International Society for Technology in Education Standards (ISTE)*. The ISTE standards for Technology Educators have been used for this book.

Another valuable feature of the book is the incorporation of many examples of social media and technology devices, strategies, processes, resources, and online teaching techniques. The information is presented in a straightforward and practical manner. The topics in this book are useful for any educator who desires to learn principles and strategies for teaching and learning more effectively with technology.

Other features of this book include:

- practical examples of social media and technology devices
- strategies for using social media to enhance learning
- approaches to designing social media programs
- strategies for maintaining a social media program
- a review of the history of social media and related technologies

Lastly, this book also contains a rich source of social media and related technology references and websites for educators. The resources provide up-to-date information on social media across the various international and national standards in technology and social media in education. This material should provide an essential foundation needed for an educator to become a skilled user of social media for the school district communications and for teaching and learning.

Chapter 1

Social Learning in a Digital Age

OBJECTIVES

At the conclusion of this chapter, you will be able to:

1. Describe what makes learning unique in a digital age (ISTE 1, 5).
2. Describe the key facets of social learning theory (ISTE 1, 5).
3. Analyze social learning theory in the context of technology progression (ISTE 7).
4. Analyze the role of technology in supporting social learning (ISTE 1, 5, 7).
5. Understand the basic components of instructional design to develop effective learning experiences using social media and collaboration tools (ISTE 1, 5).

THE DIGITAL AGE AND LEARNING

People across the world are connected now in ways that were never imagined. The Internet and the World Wide Web have become the main arteries for communication, commerce, productivity, information sharing, and data storage. Devices such as mobile phones and tablets are ubiquitous and give individuals the opportunity to accomplish tasks and communicate anywhere and anytime. Cloud-based services, smart homes, and virtual reality are now commonly discussed in mainstream news and media outlets.

Education and training have also been greatly impacted by the affordances of the web and other advances in technology. Learning, teaching, and training used to be limited by space and time. Students or trainees would walk into a brick-and-mortar school or facility at an agreed-upon date and time, sit in a desk facing a lecturer or trainer, and take notes and tests to demonstrate their learning. Now, learning is just as ubiquitous as commerce. It can happen almost anywhere, anytime, as long as an Internet connection and a computer or mobile device are available.

The range of ways that learning, teaching, and training have become digital is just as vast as the technologies that make them possible. Students can take online courses and play educational games, employees can participate in webinars and complete online tutorials, and DIYers can find videos and websites that teach them how to do anything from changing a light bulb to learning the principles of quantum physics. For those who have access to additional technologies, such as virtual reality glasses or smart televisions with webcams and motion sensors, the opportunities for next-to-real-life interactions with other individuals and with the computer itself are endless.

SOCIAL LEARNING THEORY

As the means of learning, teaching, and training have changed and grown, so have ideas about how people learn. For example, education during the Industrial Revolution involved task-focused teaching and learning, where students memorized and were tested on basic skills that would allow them to complete job-related tasks in factories, such as in math and engineering.

In the 1960s and 1970s, critics came out against the "banking" method of teaching, suggesting that knowledge is not simply something that can be moved from the teacher's brain into the student's brain and rote memorization was not a beneficial mode of learning. The answers to this problem were new theories of learning, including social learning, situated learning, and collaborative learning.

Social learning is a theory developed by social cognitive psychologist Albert Bandura (1977). This theory blends both cognitive and behavioral theories of learning (see figure 1.1). Cognitive aspects of learning include attention and memory. Behavioral aspects of learning include observing and responding to external stimuli. Motivation is another component of social learning that blends the cognitive and the behavioral.

Bandura theorized that individuals learn through observing and then imitating each other. One person serves as a model of a particular behavior. Another person observes that behavior and then carries out an interpretation of it when an appropriate situation arises or when one is motivated to do so.

To demonstrate how social learning works, specifically through observation, Bandura and colleagues (1961) videotaped adults acting out either nonaggressive or aggressive behavior toward a doll. Children observed as the adults carried out either type of behavior and then were asked to interact with

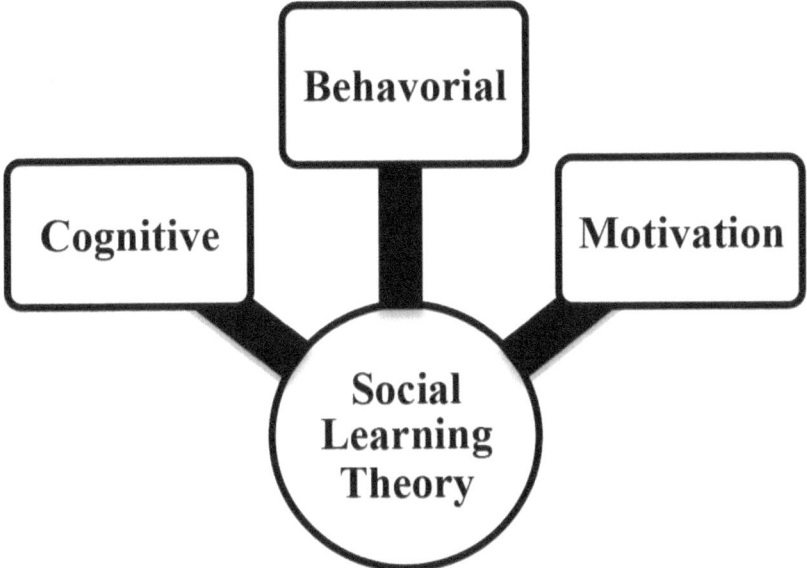

Figure 1.1. Components of social learning theory.

the doll themselves. Bandura observed that the children carried out the same behavior they had just learned from watching the adults.

Children who witnessed the violent behavior carried out violent behavior toward the doll. Children who witnessed the calm behavior carried out calm behavior toward the doll. Thus, the adults served as models for the children and, through attention, memory, and motivation, the children learned a specific behavior.

Bandura also went on to suggest that an individual's cognition and behavior inform his or her environment and vice versa. This is known as triadic reciprocal determinism (Bandura, 1978). For example, a college freshman's negative beliefs about the value of learning calculus (cognition) may lead him to not pay attention in class and perform poorly on tests (behavior). His teacher may give him a bad grade in the class, and his parents may punish him for doing poorly (social), leading him to withdraw from the class (behavior) and have a poorer view of calculus and possibly begin to devalue the college experience and his own self-efficacy (cognitive).

This model also works in the positive direction. For example, an employee may desire a salary increase (cognitive), so she works extra hard at completing a project before the deadline (behavior). Her boss rewards her with a salary increase and praise at a meeting, leading her coworkers to congratulate her and express their support (social). She may now continue to demonstrate proactive behaviors at work, not just for future raises, but because she appreciates the praise and feels more confident in her abilities.

Several studies have demonstrated the application of social learning theory across disciplines. In a study of prediabetic patients, researchers found that external influences such as social support and medical professional actions (social) as well as the patient's specific beliefs about self-care (cognitive) affected the patient's self-care to prevent full-blown diabetes (behavior) (Chen, Wang, & Hung, 2015).

Another study of supervisors and work group members demonstrated how ethical leadership (social) contributes to the working group's learning behaviors (behavior) and shared perceptions of the fairness with which they treat each other (cognitive) (Walumbwa, Hartnell, & Misati, 2017).

When studying bullying through a social learning lens, researchers found that children who witness bullying behavior (social) have a belief that bullying is okay (cognitive), and those who carry out bullying behaviors (behavior) but do not receive punishment (social) will continue to demonstrate bullying behaviors (Swearer, Wang, Berry, & Myers, 2014).

Social learning theory also translates well into a classroom or training situation. When individuals meet in person, they can model processes and concepts for each other and enact them. For example, a teacher can work a math problem on the board and then ask a student to demonstrate the same problem-solving steps she used, providing guidance along the way. If individuals are not in the same location, they can still learn from each other and give support and constructive criticism through electronic verbal communication.

They can follow step-by-step instructions spoken to them or written down in a guide and provide written or verbal feedback on a finished product. Lastly, individuals can learn from each other through symbolic means, such as through a video or picture. For example, if a plumber's apprentice wants to learn how to fix a leaky faucet, he can watch a video of an expert completing the same task.

Bandura's social learning theory is just the tip of the iceberg when it comes to theories about how people learn from and with each other. There are additional theories similar to or that build upon social learning theory including social constructivism, apprenticeship, situated learning, and computer-supported collaborative learning. Some of these are referenced later in this book (see figure 1.2).

HOW IS SOCIAL LEARNING THEORY RELEVANT TODAY?

Social learning is relevant now in the digital age more than ever because people are sharing information and communicating at a pace and in a volume

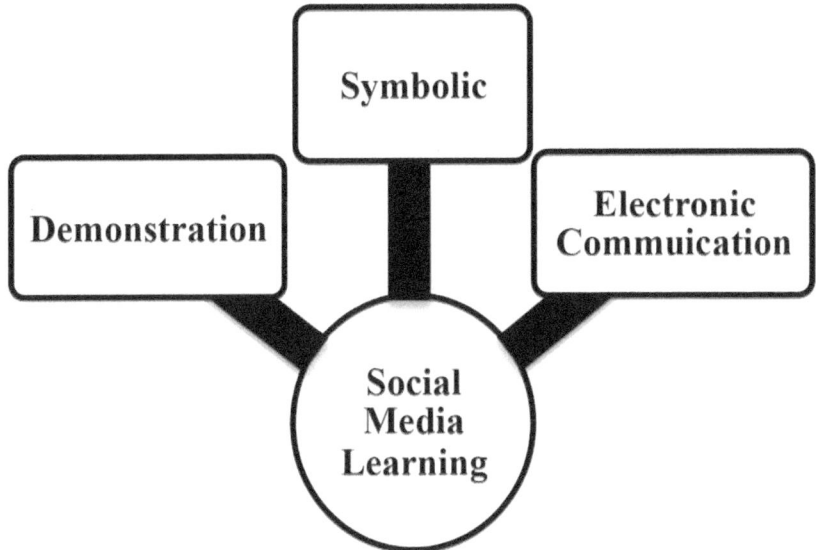

Figure 1.2. Types of learning through social media.

unmatched by any other time in history. Technologies such as the internet and the mobile phone have made social exchanges much easier, quicker, and wider reaching. This rapid progress of technologies means there are many more opportunities for social learning to occur and be supported.

Students and learners of all types have many more opportunities to learn from each other during these social exchanges, whether they are intentionally seeking out that learning or they are casually browsing and become accidental learners. In addition, individuals using the internet have access to many more experts, leaders, and teachers than they would with analog or non-digital means of communication.

As a result of these changes, there is much more opportunity for social learning to occur both in cyberspace and in real life. Educators and trainers can support social learning in their learning spaces by developing activities and strategies that involve more social exchange, modeling, observation, and the use of social technologies to afford these practices.

Software and application developers can design more tools that facilitate social learning. Students and employees can reinvent the ways they communicate outside of school or work to engage with each other on school- or work-related matters. It is imperative that the power of technology for social learning be harnessed for the benefit of all who are in learning or training situations.

Two types of tools that have allowed for more social interaction via digital means are social media tools and collaboration tools. Facebook, Skype, and

Slack are just few examples of tools that allow for both formal and informal learning, as well as structured and unstructured learning. These tools, their features, and their advantages and disadvantages will be discussed in later chapters. Additionally, since simply using a tool does not lead to social learning, strategies and activities for using them for social learning will be discussed as well.

PREPARING FOR LEARNING AND INSTRUCTION

Understanding the tools, features, and learning activities and strategies of social learning is key to facilitation. However, just as important is understanding how to prepare and employ them for effective learning instruction. Figure 1.3 describes some of the basic strategies of preparing for the learning instruction that involves social media and collaboration tools.

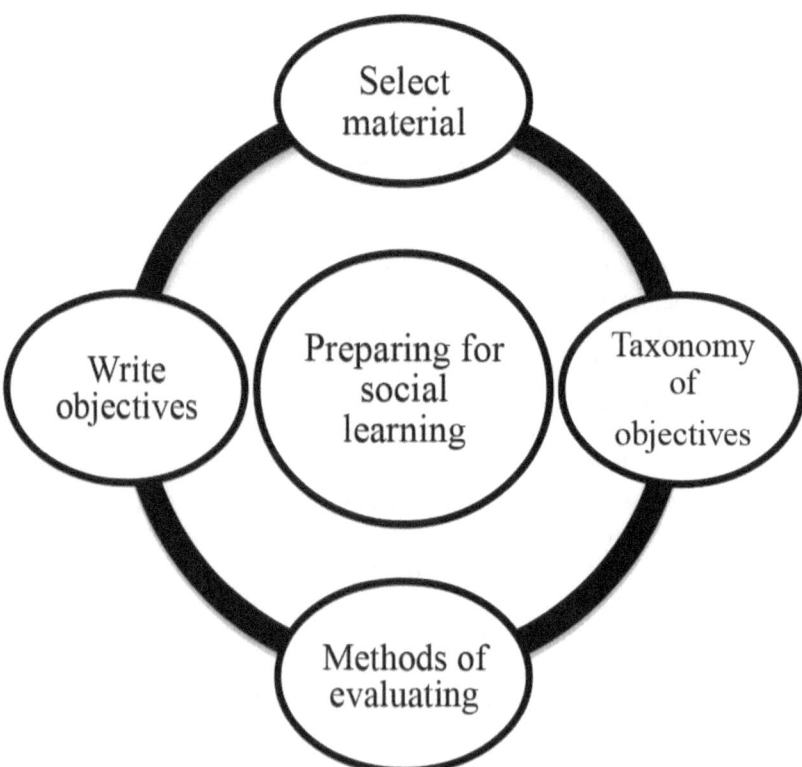

Figure 1.3. Examples of preparing for social learning.

In preparing for collaborative learning, remember the phrase "Those who fail to plan, plan to fail." Some examples of poor planning for learning include:

1. Not understanding what you're trying to accomplish
2. Mistakes on screens and documents
3. Lack of selection or wrong selection of media
4. Inadequate technology applications or material
5. Lack of prior planning of logistics with learners
6. Inadequate planning of time allotment, or disorganization
7. Failure to properly assess the learners and match material
8. Poor outline or objectives
9. Failure to keep learners engaged and motivated
10. Failure to design the social media framework
11. Not understanding the learners' needs
12. Not understanding the technology

Using the reverse of the preceding list as a checklist for "ideal planning" is another way to look at this issue. Planning involves looking at the whole picture of the learning experience, often starting with assessing the needs of the learner and the learning environment.

A critical part of planning is assessing the learner's knowledge, behavior, or performance and what gaps or problems exist that need to be addressed. It is also important to assess the learning environment and resources. Examples include:

1. *Experience:* An old adage applies here; never underestimate the intelligence of your participants and never overestimate their need for information. Do you need to do a needs assessment? What is the knowledge level of the learners in using technology and social media?
2. *Interest:* If you have the learner's interest working for you from the beginning, the success of your session is 50 percent assured. Even if interest is lacking initially, it can be built by skillful use of strategies. You must be able to engage your learners.
3. *Terminology:* Terminology can be extremely tricky for the facilitator who is an expert on the topic. Nothing loses the learners faster than the use of technical jargon they don't understand. The problem takes on greater complexity when several topics are involved.
4. *Background:* What is the background of the participants? Who has the most influence in this group? Sometimes there are key people in the session. What problems and personal interests do these people have?
5. *Technical environment:* Don't fail to assess the technical environment. You will need to ensure the learners have the appropriate technology

for the social media learning session. What do the learners expect of you—a deeply serious, technical session or an informal discussion of the problem?

The next stage of planning involves identifying the type of learning experience that will occur, the learner audience, details of the experience, and expectations. Once you have a good idea of the learners, before you begin preparing a session, find out as much as you can about:

1. The type of session you will be expected to give
   - classroom instruction
   - training workshop
   - eLearning module or course
   - webinar
   - self-guided tutorial
   - formal presentation
   - informal presentation

2. The composition of the learners
   - students
   - learners (company)
   - client (session tailored to customer)

3. The time allotted for the session
   - a long session provides more freedom to explore your topic
   - a short session needs to be very clear, addressing the topic directly

4. The expectations for session
   - Is there a specific purpose for session?
   - Clarify the expectations beforehand and address them during the session.
   - Will concepts be new to this audience or building upon their prior knowledge?
   - Do you need formal assessments or accreditation documentation?

Once you have a general idea of what you want to do, you'll have to decide how to do it. It is essential that your session has a well-constructed outline and lesson plan (i.e., facilitator's notes). Some strategies include:

1. Prepare far in advance.
2. Submit beforehand to appropriate stakeholders.

3. Identify and list the issues you plan to address and arrange them in a logical sequence.
4. Determine transition elements that will help your audience to follow the linkage from one point to the other.
5. Prepare your equipment, handouts, materials, and supplies.

Organizing and selecting content, materials, and resources is the next step. Make sure all the content is relevant to the session and is well organized. Whether you are giving a technical session or preparing for a discussion activity using social media, you will need to structure the material and content in an organized and logical manner. Some techniques for organizing content include:

1. *Degree of acceptance:* Beginning with what will learners accept as important or true, have trouble accepting, and need more time and deliberation to accept.
2. *Level of difficulty/familiarity:* Beginning with what will learners already know and what will they need more information on to proceed.
3. *Incremental:* Working up from basic to more advanced topics and concepts in small steps.
4. *Chronological approach:* Taking learners through information or a process according to how it occurs in time.
5. *Analysis method:* Deconstructing topics or concepts into subtopics and sub-concepts for better understanding.
6. *Synthesis method:* Identifying and evaluating similarities and differences among topics and concepts to construct new meaning.
7. *Topical approach:* Breaking up larger concepts and topics into sub-concepts or subtopics.
8. *Hierarchical:* Identifying the guiding or overarching principles, guidelines, and concepts and exploring their components or criteria.
9. *Instruct "Must Know" content first (see figure 1.4):* Some examples of the "Must Know" content are listed in table 1.1. The priority should start with the *must know* material first and *nice to know* material last depending upon time.

Another critical step in planning an instructional design is writing learning objectives. Learning objectives are sometimes called learning goals and are often written in one or two sentences. They are tied to outcomes and assessments, activities, and readings or resources used in a learning experience. They help all stakeholders recognize the reason "why" the learning experience is taking place.

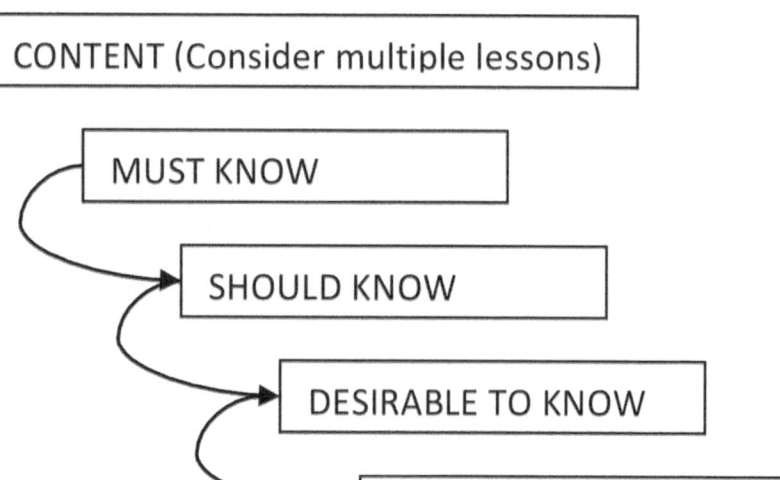

Figure 1.4. Prioritizing content for learning.

Table 1.1. Example of Structuring a Learning Experience with the "Must Know" Technique

Objective	Instruction
Must Know	Operate a cell phone
Should Know	Proper care of the cell phone
Desirable to Know	Optional features of cell phone
Nice to Know	Inventor and evolution of the cell phone

According to Robert Mager (1984), behavioral objectives must incorporate the following components:

1. *Subject:* The topic, subject area, knowledge area, discipline, or content.
2. *Measurable:* The learning or learner must be able to be assessed through quantitative or qualitative means, such as a grade, score, frequency of occurrence, or written evaluation.
3. *Level of Performance:* The learner's performance should be apparent and the level should fall on a continuum, such as novice to expert or does not meet to meets expectations.
4. *Condition:* The environment or conditions under which the learner performs should be identified.

It is also important to select the level in Bloom's (1956) *Taxonomy of Objectives* so that it is clear whether the learning is foundational or higher level. A description of each level in the hierarchy is listed in table 1.2. In the description for each level are some sample words that can be used in a learning objective statement, such as "Can *recognize* the differences between profit and revenue when analyzing the financial structure of a business."

Included with the learning objectives or in an instructional design plan is often an acknowledgment of the type of domain in which a learning experience exists. Bloom's (1956) three major domains are listed in table 1.3. Most learning experiences incorporate one of these, though some have a mix. Identifying where the learning experience falls relative to the learning objective will help drive the design.

Another key component in designing a learning experience is evaluation. Kirkpatrick (1994) identified four levels of evaluation that are critical for

Table 1.2. Levels of Bloom's Taxonomy

Level	Description
1. Knowledge	*Ability to recall or memorize.* Common verbs include acquire, select, state, recall, count, locate, identify, recognize, memorize, and reproduce.
2. Comprehension	*Ability to understand meaning of material.* Common verbs include associate, draw, expand, conclude, explain, compare, record, express, infer, represent, and differentiate.
3. Application	*Ability to apply or use the material.* Common verbs include apply, determine, classify, practice, construct, solve, estimate, expand, demonstrate, and interact.
4. Analysis	*Ability to break down into components.* Common verbs include arrange, breakdown, subdivide, discriminate, transform, differentiate, formulate, and sort.
5. Synthesis	*Ability to put components back together.* Common verbs include arrange, build, develop, combine, modify, produce, synthesis, reconstruct, reorganize, deduct, and create.
6. Evaluation	*Ability to process critical judgment or assessment.* Common verbs include appraise, determine, interpret, validate, judge, defend, conclude, justify, test, and evaluate.

Table 1.3. Bloom's Domains of Instruction and Learning

Domain	Description
1. Cognitive	*Instruction that focuses on mental learning.* Examples include command of information and knowledge, comprehension, applying, analyzing, synthesizing, and evaluating.
2. Affective	*Instruction that focuses on feeling, values, and emotions.* Examples include receiving, responding, valuing, organizing, and characterizing.
3. Psychomotor	*Instruction that focuses on physical skill development.* Examples include operating equipment, repairing, building, setting, adapting, and originating.

determining the effectiveness and efficiency of learning or training designs. Most instructional designs touch on at least one of the following:

1. *Reaction:* Did they enjoy the session?
2. *Learning:* Did they learn content and understand it?
3. *Behavior:* Did they develop new skills?
4. *Results:* Can they transfer the knowledge skills and apply them?

These four levels of evaluation can be assessed using a variety of instruments (see table 1.4). In a social learning setting, learners might be assessed with a combination of instruments, such as observations, self- or peer-evaluations, or role-play. Determining the type of instruments for assessment and evaluation of learning objectives when planning the learning experience will help determine the activities, resources, and content needed for successful learning.

Lastly, you've probably heard this before, but that doesn't diminish its importance. Practice is important. No matter how rushed you might be, make time for at least a few practice runs and get familiar with the technology and applications.

1. Try navigating using the material and technology and ensure it all works well. Ask for feedback, and then act on that information.
2. Run through your key presentations or content one more time.
3. Review all the learning material used in the session.
4. Make sure needed equipment is available to learners and facilitators and working properly.
5. Pay particular attention to the appearance of the screens and content. Avoid crowded material and screens and follow design guidelines where applicable.

Table 1.4. Instruments for Assessment

Instrument	Measures
1. Pretests and posttests	Learning
2. Video observation	Behavior
3. Work reports/performance	Skills and results
4. Questionnaires	Perceptions
5. Interviews	Perception/behaviors
6. Self- or peer evaluations	Change perception
7. Job/task completions	Performances/skills
8. Portfolios	Development process
9. Rubrics	Comparison
10. Essay, case studies	High-level learning
11. Multiple choice	Learning
12. Critical incidents, role-play	Skills and learning

SUMMARY

The development of digital media and tools continues to pave the path for instructional design and learning. Learners and learning facilitators can interact with each other and with information oftentimes more efficiently and more effectively than ever before. While some technologies have enhanced face-to-face interactions, other technologies have replaced the need for face-to-face interactions. Thus, the popularity of computer-supported and fully online learning has increased.

As these technologies have grown in number and capabilities, it is critical to think about their role in terms of learning theories. Social learning theory continues to be a foundational theory for understanding learning in general, but it is particularly important to consider in terms of learning with and through technology. Many of the claims that have been made about social learning in face-to-face classroom and training situations also apply to situations that are virtual or digital. Social media and collaboration tools are just two types of technologies that allow for successful social learning to happen in the digital age.

It may seem that social media and collaboration tools would change teaching and learning practices. Some changes can be made to practice to ensure learners are engaged, learning, and using the tools most effectively. These will be discussed in this book. However, there are some strategies for designing learning experiences that need not change to accommodate these new tools. Planning, writing learning objectives, using Bloom's taxonomy and domains, and integrating assessment and evaluation strategies are key practices that all educators, trainers, instructional designers, curriculum designers, and other learning facilitators should implement for successful learning.

EXERCISES

Exercise 1. Instructional Design Prospectus

In this exercise, you will propose the design of a learning experience such as a webinar, face-to-face training, online course, grade school unit/lesson, or workshop that is informed by social learning. The design must also have a specific, real-world purpose and audience, such as "a webinar that will educate 100 employees about a new timesheet completion procedure" or "an online workshop that will guide high school juniors in the college or job-hunting process."

In your prospectus, please include the following:

I. Overview (design type, goals, learning objectives, and potential difficulties):

  a. Design problem and goals should include statements about (1) why you are designing this experience, (2) who the design/technology is serving (the learner group), (3) what problem it is solving, and (4) how you believe the learning experience will assist to resolve that specific problem through social learning. The context and the need for the learning design or technology should be clearly articulated.

b. Design Type: Explain the category of design you have in mind (workshop, lesson, webinar, app, etc.). Explain how you believe this learning experience will solve the problem and meet your goals through social learning.

c. Learning Objectives: One of the most important aspects of instructional design is to include the learning objectives. Use action verbs from Bloom's taxonomy to write at least two sentences that explain what the learners should be able to do, know, and/or understand by the end of the learning experience. These objectives should be directly tied to the goals and design problem you articulated earlier.

d. Difficulties: List difficulties that might emerge throughout the development and implementation of the design.

II. What's Been Done?: A review or summary of at least five similar learning experiences, systems, or technologies that might provide some insight into your design. Make connections with other designs currently available in the market. Please provide links to these designs where appropriate.

III. What's Been Said?: A brief list and a one to two sentence summary of five scholarly articles, case studies, or research studies that you believe relate to the type of learning experience or technology you are designing. These must be tied to your goals and design type. Please make sure to include at least five research citations that describe how your proposed project includes elements and/or features already described in the academic literature. Please make sure you identify (one to two sentences) how each article or study relates to your proposed design.

IV. Innovative Ideas: Include at least five "innovative ideas" that represent creative solutions or functions that are "outside the box" when it comes to instructional design and technology. Ensure there is an appropriate fit between the technology and nature of the problem. For instance, proposing that Facebook be used to submit a federally regulated document would not be acceptable.

V. Bibliography/Reference List (APA format): Include the full bibliographic entry for any source you cited in the preceding sections

Exercise 2. Instructional Design Plan

Identify a need or problem in your organization or institution that would require the development of a learning experience involving social learning. If you completed exercise 1, you may use that prospectus as your basis for this exercise. Follow the guidance in this chapter and respond to the questions that follow to draft an instructional design plan.

- What learning tasks need to be completed through this experience for learners to meet the learning objectives you listed in your prospectus? (Complete readings, watch videos, successfully pass quizzes, complete team project, write a reflection, etc.)
- How long will each task take? (minutes, hours, days, etc.)
- What content will be incorporated in the instructional design? List titles of specific videos, slides, assignments, activities, assessments, quizzes. It is okay if you do not have these fully written out or developed. That is something a subject matter expert (SME) usually does, but please at least list/title the content you "intend" to be incorporated in the experience.
- How will learners interact with the content and activities? Will you put the content in a free learning management system (LMS)? Will it be a public website? Will it be a narrated slideshow with links to external chat and quiz programs? Will it be a guided tutorial available for completion on an organization's website?
- How will learners navigate the learning experience? Will it be facilitator-led and timed? Will they browse through a course menu? Will they click a single "Go" button with "Next" buttons? Will an agenda, handouts, and technology resources be provided ahead of time?
- List the scaffolds and activities of the learning experience: Will it be branched so learners can choose their own path or will it be linear or sequential? Will there be small-group, large-group, or independent activities? How much interaction will the facilitator have? Provide an outline, flowchart, or agenda of the activities that comprise the learning experience.
- What additional tools, software, or other resources are needed for the design to be implemented? Some examples include videos, websites, apps, social media tools, collaboration tools, a learner roster/database, an e-mail system, a computer lab with Wi-Fi, textbook or manuals, and an instructor/facilitator guide.

REFERENCES

Bandura, A. (1977). *Social learning theory.* New York: General Learning Press.
——— (1978). The self system in reciprocal determinism. *American Psychologist, 33*(4), 344.
Bandura, A., Ross, D., & Ross, S. A. (1961). Transmission of aggression through imitation of aggressive models. *Journal of Abnormal and Social Psychology, 63,* 575–582.

Bloom, B. S. (1956). *Taxonomy of educational objectives, Handbook I: The cognitive domain*. New York: David McKay Co Inc.

Chen, M. F., Wang, R. H., & Hung, S. L. (2015). Predicting health-promoting self-care behaviors in people with pre-diabetes by applying Bandura social learning theory. *Applied Nursing Research, 28*(4), 299–304.

Kirkpatrick, D. (1994). *Evaluating training programs: The four levels*. San Francisco: Berrett-Koehler.

Mager, R. F. (1984). *Preparing instructional objectives*. (2nd ed.). Belmont, CA: David S. Lake.

Swearer, S. M., Wang, C., Berry, B., & Myers, Z. R. (2014). Reducing bullying: Application of social cognitive theory. *Theory into Practice, 53*(4), 271–277.

Walumbwa, F. O., Hartnell, C. A., & Misati, E. (2017). Does ethical leadership enhance group learning behavior? Examining the mediating influence of group ethical conduct, justice climate, and peer justice. *Journal of Business Research, 72*, 14–23.

Chapter 2

Social Learning Theories and Models

OBJECTIVES

At the conclusion of this chapter, you will be able to:

1. Describe the key aspects of social learning theories and other social constructivism (ISTE 1).
2. Describe the significance of two social learning frameworks that are informed by social learning theories: legitimate peripheral participation and cognitive apprenticeship (ISTE 1).
3. Evaluate and apply the above theories and frameworks in an effort to develop social learning experiences inside and outside of the classroom as well as in face-to-face and digital interactions (ISTE 1, 5, 6).

SOCIAL LEARNING THEORIES

People learn through social interaction. A variety of social media and collaboration tools make this interaction more effective and efficient. There are many strategies for teaching and learning with social media and collaboration tools. However, it is important to first learn about the learning theories that inform their use for this purpose such as those listed in figure 2.1.

Many of today's educators, trainers, and researchers would say that all learning is social by nature, though there are some who continue to promote instructionist, behaviorist, objectivist, and banking learning theories and models. These theories and models are primarily focused on the individual's ability to make meaning and how knowledge is "transmitted" through various means; the social aspects are not at the forefront of discussion.

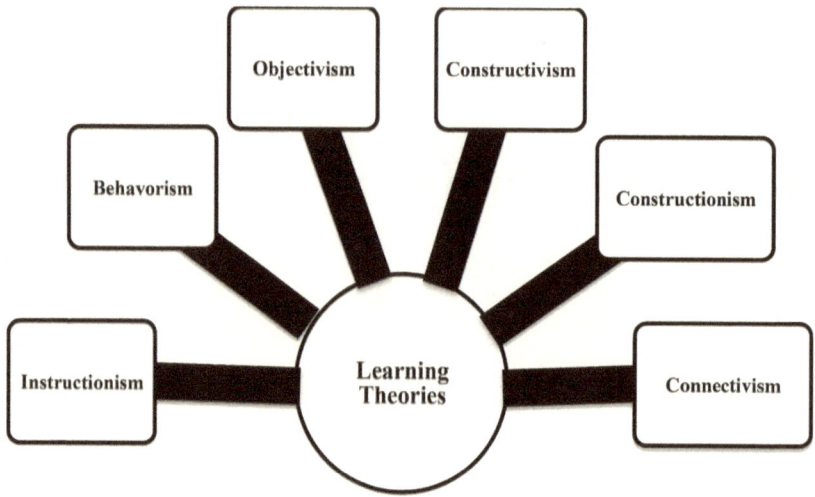

Figure 2.1. Examples of learning theories.

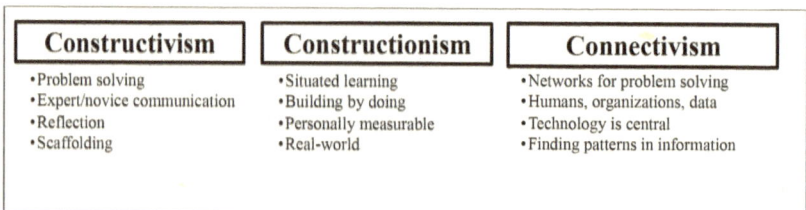

Figure 2.2. Basics of constructivism, constructionism, connectivism.

Those who focus more on the social aspects and benefits of learning believe that no one learns in a vacuum. Knowledge is constructed and meaning is made through interaction with others, and it is through facilitating or harnessing the social aspects of learning that people learn best. Social learning is one example of a learning theory that supports these beliefs, which was discussed in chapter 1.

Additional foundational learning theories that support beliefs about social learning include constructivism and, in the case of technology-supported social learning, constructionism and connectivism (see figure 2.2). Additionally, two related frameworks, legitimate peripheral participation and cognitive apprenticeship, are fundamental to how people learn with and through each other. These will be discussed in this chapter.

It makes sense to discuss these theories when thinking about social media and collaboration tools for learning, especially since these tools are, in fact, designed for social interaction. Having a strong understanding of these will create the foundation for better design of learning experiences that are truly beneficial for the learner using the tools we have available to us today.

CONSTRUCTIVISM

Those who consider themselves "constructivists" believe that learning is not a transmission of information from one source to another in a classroom environment, which is processed and stored in the brain, and then ready for use when needed. Instead, it is a dynamic social activity that occurs in diverse situations, in a variety of ways, and with diverse players, with an understanding that different people learn differently.

While there is not one single explanation for how people learn best, there are several established best practices involved in the learning process that align with constructivism. One is establishing authentic situations where identity construction and problem solving can take place. Another is the creation of opportunities for participation in communities of experts as well as modeling of and reflection upon processes and strategies. Lastly, higher-level or expert ways of thinking about common situations and problems can be scaffolded by a teacher or facilitator.

Jean Piaget's (1983) philosophy of constructivism centers around the idea that individuals construct meaning and knowledge through their unique social experiences via assimilation and accommodation. As opposed to "instructionism," "constructivism" is about ways of knowing—or epistemologies—rather than acquisition of knowledge. Lev Vygotsky (1978) followed suit by proposing the concept of the zone of proximal development (ZPD) in learning situations.

This aspect of constructivism focuses on the understanding that individuals learn through a process of collaboration and scaffolding provided by a teacher or other facilitator. Then, as the learner gains more expertise within the ZPD, the scaffolds can be incrementally taken away.

Educator and researcher Barbara Rogoff (1994) took the idea of constructivism further and stated that "learning is a process of transformation of participation itself . . . how people develop is a function of their transforming roles and understanding in the activities in which they participate" (p. 209). Through a theory of participation lens, she set out to show that designing learning experiences aligned with constructivism was more beneficial for learners than those that follow the more "instructionist" perspective.

In her research, Rogoff (1994) analyzed two one-sided models of learning: (1) transmission: learning is transmitted from expert to novice and (2) acquisition: knowledge is discovered through interaction with peers and others—with a community-of-learners model "in which responsibility and autonomy are both desired [and] learning is transforming participation in shared sociocultural endeavors" (p. 210). The type of participation in the process of learning leads to a different relation to the subject matter and to the community that sees it as important.

In Rogoff's observations of a middle-class Euro-American mother and child and a Mayan mother and child: the former was often involved in solo and didactic activities, which followed a traditional schooling model, while the latter was involved in integrated community activities. In the example of the Mayan mother and child, the learners, parents, and teachers all participate in learning together in a community, and even newcomers are learning through participation in the integrated community activities. This example shows that becoming part of a community of learners is inherent in the process of learning and sets the stage for success for the learner when a constructivist approach is taken.

Constructivism is a well-known and popular learning theory that most learning facilitators follow in their practice today. It can be applied widely to a variety of learning situations, with or without additional resources and learning tools. In essence, the only "resource" needed for success in learning according to constructivists is the learning community.

CONSTRUCTIONISM

Constructionism is an extension of constructivism. As shown in figure 2.3, this theory asserts the belief that learning happens when an individual reconstructs knowledge in a situated, public way ("situated learning") and by

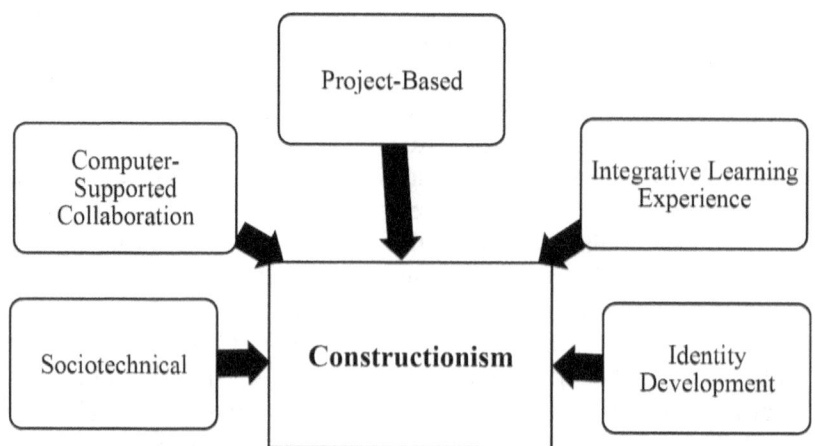

Figure 2.3. Constructionist principles.

building or doing things that are personally meaningful to the learner and in the real world with experts and models as guides (Papert & Harel, 1991).

To demonstrate constructionism at work, Papert and Harel (1991) created an *Instructional Software Design Project* (ISDP), where they asked a fourth-grade class to design and produce software to teach younger students about fractions. This project supports a constructionist model in that it encourages not only "learning by doing," but also thinking and talking about what you do. Furthermore, it supports social constructionism because the learning was happening with a social situation in mind (students teaching other students while being mentored by teachers).

The major components of the fourth-graders' projects included lab time, focus sessions, demos, and the crafting of a designer notebook. Methods included pre- and posttests for the control (no computers), experiment group A (computers without ISDP), and ISDP, observation, interviews, and students' work. The authors wished to show, with some level of rigor, that learning took place, what and how they learned, and why they learned what they learned.

In the end, the students in the class who learned through a constructionist approach were able to work better on their computers and did better on their tests regarding domain knowledge (fractions). They were also able to manage tasks, processes, metacognitive awareness, and problems.

Social learning through design of learning artifacts played a role here, especially in the interactions between the learner and leader/teacher, who shared her own designs with the fourth-graders. The demos were another example of social learning through design where fourth-graders demonstrated their software with third-graders. In addition, the fact that students were constructing a "real" artifact for a "real" audience lends itself to Papert and Harel's later work on situating constructionism, which discusses the role of personally meaningful activities that build on one's existing knowledge as contributing to improvement in performance.

Many learning technologies have been developed that reflect constructionist theory. For example, in her research, Marina Bers (2001) showed how ten specific features of constructionist-inspired sociotechnical systems called identity construction environments (ICEs) can be useful in supporting positive youth development. Her theoretical model, rooted in constructionist theory, demonstrated how the role of learners' multifaceted identity and their ability to represent that identity in computer-constructed, project-based learning situations can augment integrative learning.

One ICE that she designed and studied was called Zora. It was an identity construction environment that allowed children to create digital objects such as avatars, buildings, signs, symbols, food, books, events, and institutions. Zora objects represent elements that make up an identity in a virtual community. Bers investigated Zora objects as a means of gaining a better understanding of the role of personal and moral values in a community.

The design of Zora followed a constructionist approach because it not only allowed students to create real artifacts to represent themselves and discuss real issues with others, but it also allowed students to construct their own curricula. In other words, students work together to construct projects that are personally meaningful to them.

Features of Zora that support project-based, constructionist learning include: (1) an object-oriented system allowing users to create representations of identity such as avatars, photo albums, and environmental elements that support personal narrative/storytelling; (2) collaborative tools for creation and participation in a community; (3) an authoring layer that is easy to use for novices; (4) evaluation tools; and (5) a 3D interface similar to video games (see figure 2.4).

Project-based learning environments such as Zora also support constructionism and motivate students because learners are engaged in solving real problems, creating authentic and public artifacts, and socializing with others about these problems and projects. Zora supports both the cognitive (content and skills) as well as the metacognitive (Blomenfeld & Soloway, 1991).

However, sustaining motivation is only possible through careful pedagogical planning and understanding. Teachers need to support students in learning ways of thinking, assess what they already know, scaffold academic and cognitively challenging tasks, and maintain an environment that encourages risk-taking rather than getting it right. Technology also plays an important role in constructionist project-based learning because it provides access to information and people/community, allows for greater choice and control, is interactive, and can be manipulated for different skill levels via scaffolding (Blomenfeld & Soloway, 1991).

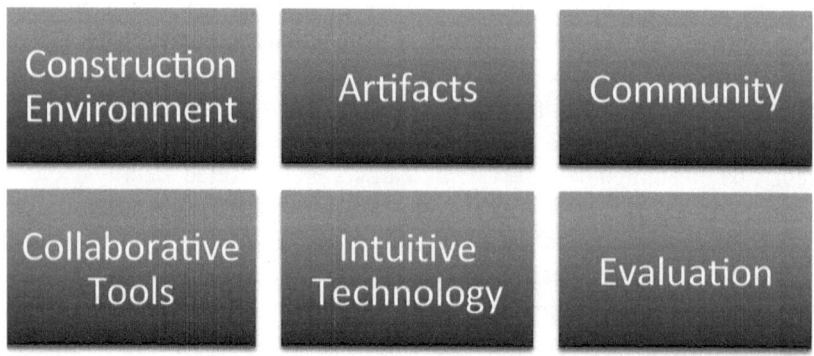

Figure 2.4. Constructionist resources.

If social constructivism is learning through social interaction, constructionism is learning through meaning-making with others plus the development or construction of artifacts that reflect that social meaning-making. In both the ISDP and the ICE cases described above, the learners constructed meaning together, constructed their learning communities together, and constructed an artifact to reflect their identities, learning, and communities together. In both cases, we also see evidence of the learners following a participatory or an apprenticeship framework, which is described further in the Legitimate Peripheral Participation and Cognitive Apprenticeship sections below.

LEGITIMATE PERIPHERAL PARTICIPATION

Legitimate peripheral participation and cognitive apprenticeship theories support the notion that learning happens through interactions with others, scaffolding, development of learning communities, and creation of artifacts that reflect learning. In the last few decades, educational researchers have looked closer at the activity that happens in these communities and in the ZPD, and have learned more about the significance of the roles of the expert and the apprentice, and the ways that learning happens as individuals participate in these communities (Chaiklin, 2003).

Lave and Wenger (1991) observed tailors, butchers, and recovering alcoholics in their respective learning communities. They found that novices learned not through direct instruction and "how-to," but through exposure to experts' practices in the communities in-situ.

For example, a butcher learns the terminology, techniques, communication styles, and common practices of the profession peripherally and incrementally; yet, authentically, first by taking on peripheral tasks and interacting with other members in the learning community (other novices, experts, indirect members of the community). Through this exposure, novices learn the meanings, practices, and rules of their communities. Although the novices are not fully participating in the community, this legitimate peripheral participation (LPP) is a form of learning.

As mentioned already, Rogoff (1994) encountered similar learning through LPP when observing Mayan mothers and their children, noting that their introduction to practice in the community was not through one-on-one didactic instruction from mom, but through exposure to authentic practices, rules, and community interactions on a daily basis with many community members.

In an LPP scenario, there is a continuum from novice to expert, and learners are exposed to the work of the expert in an indirect, or "peripheral," way. Experts not only have more knowledge but also can access knowledge, apply knowledge, organize and maintain flexibility with knowledge and concepts,

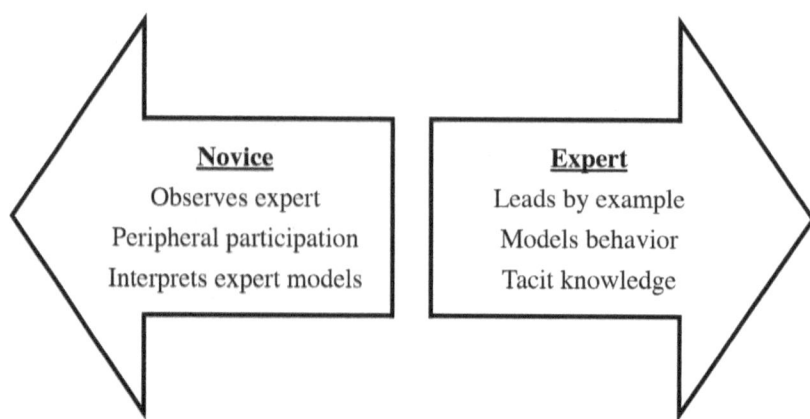

Figure 2.5. Novice to expert continuum.

and are able to identify patterns more easily than novices (Donovan, Bransford, & Pellegrino, 1999). See figure 2.5.

The problem is that experts often have a hard time articulating or directly teaching this information to novices in a way that facilitates learning. To maximize learning, suggestions for helping novices gain expertise include coaching by experts, integrating activities that include models of how experts handle problems, focusing on "conditionalized knowledge" (applications of knowledge), and being intentionally and openly metacognitive about the learning process (pp. 49–50).

COGNITIVE APPRENTICESHIP

Similar to legitimate peripheral participation, cognitive apprenticeship refers to the application of workplace apprentice-type learning but in traditional schooling environments. The goal is to place more emphasis on the methods and processes that experts understand and use when solving problems. Experts must also carry out tasks in specific domains so that learners can apply the same methods/processes when they encounter problems or situations.

This differs from textbook problems and issues students encounter in the classroom (Collins, Brown, & Newman, 1989). Teachers should aim for "externalization of processes that are usually carried out internally" (p. 457). This type of teaching, reflecting Vygotsky's (1978) ZPD, involves (1) modeling (observation of the "master" using cognitive and metacognitive processes and comparison to one's own practice), (2) coaching (practice of those processes with guidance and feedback from the "master"), and (3) gradual "fading" of the master's intervention.

Collins, Brown, and Newman (1989) describe the following examples of social constructionist practices, such as LPP and cognitive apprenticeship.

1. To teach reading, Palincsar and Brown (1986) implemented their "Reciprocal Teaching" method, which invites learners to learn a higher-level process and method for reading: formulating questions, summarizing, clarifying, and predicting what will come next. The teacher models this process for the students first, encouraging learners to compare their process to hers. The teacher also must scaffold elements of this process for students and support them in being both "the producer and the critic."
2. Scardamalia and Bereiter's (1984) teaching of writing involves procedural supports such as prompts for generating ideas and revising them (soloing) when writing as well as reflecting upon the choices they wind up making and whether they are successful in meeting their higher-level goals, self-monitoring, and self-correction (coinvestigation).
3. In teaching math, Schoenfeld (1985) found that teachers or coaches working with students on a series of heuristics, control strategies, and belief systems that apply generally to math problems helped them become better at problem solving.

Collins, Brown, and Newman (1989) note, "Seeing how experts deal with problems that are difficult for them is critical to students' developing a belief in their own capabilities" (473).

One final example demonstrates cognitive apprenticeship in an adult learning situation. In his research, Donald Schon (1987) discusses the role of reflection-in-action and reflection on reflection-in-action in a coach–student learning experience. Namely, he envisions a reflective practicum that centers on learning while doing, the dynamic relationship between learner and coach, and the tacit knowledge that lends itself to the "artistry" in the professions that cannot be "taught" in the traditional ways we think of teaching. He also places a juxtaposition on technical rationality and research in terms of learning theory vs. knowing practice.

Examples that demonstrate this reflective practice via cognitive apprenticeship include the architect studio, counseling, psychoanalytic practice, and music instruction (see figure 2.6). In these situations, much of the learning goes on through dialogue, imitation, opening oneself to new perspectives, listening, and demonstrating between learner and coach.

Schon (1987) notes that the dialogue between coach and student happens in a variety of ways. The student is learning to design but is also learning how to learn through telling/listening, demonstrating, and imitating. The student must "suspend disbelief" since she does not yet know the expert processes or the meaning of what she is doing, and must learn the coach's dialogue and

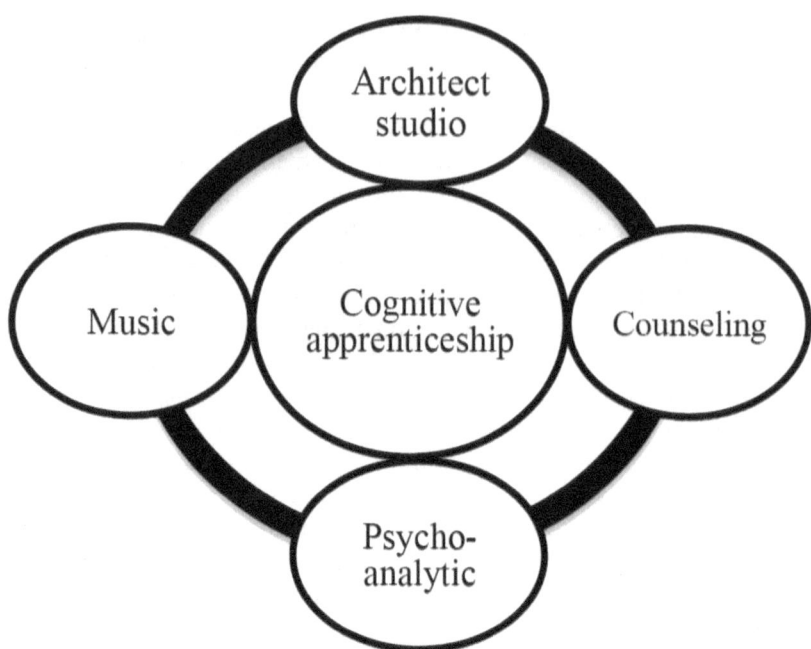

Figure 2.6. Examples of cognitive apprenticeship in practice.

listen as she designs. However, the coach and student must engage in reciprocal reflection-in-action, reflecting on the practice as well as the practicum and their dialogues, definitions, and understandings of each other.

It is possible, though, that the student does not want to "suspend disbelief" and refuses to give up her independence and self-reliance (does not want to be under coach's authority). This is when the coach and student cannot come to an understanding of each other's language. They have not reflected on meaning underlying questions, interactions, and dialogue. Their perspectives and views are incongruent.

To aid in reflection-in-action on the theories in use by both parties, the coach can legitimize the student's desires for a project, encourage production, and open up possibilities with quick examples (coexperimentation), and assess the work in terms of the qualities the student defined at the outset.

Cognitive apprenticeship may seem like a fancy name for many common learning interactions everyone has experienced. However, assigning this name to it makes it clear that when people learn, especially in traditional classroom environments, they are not learning only due to their own capacity for learning or because of their individual interest.

Nor are they learning as a result of interactions with peers who are just like them or at the same level as them. In any learning scenario, the presence of a peer, coach, expert, or other learning facilitator makes an impact. They provide feedback, demonstrate expert processes, help learners reflect on learning, and walk them through worked or annotated examples. This will lead to a more successful learning experience.

CONNECTIVISM

The learning theories discussed so far have tended to focus on learning as a process that happens within the individual learner. Siemens (2005) found that this was too limited of a perspective because the theories did not address the role of organizational learning. He also argued that learning processes have taken on new characteristics as a result of the exponential development of technology in the twenty-first century. Thus, he coined a new learning theory called *connectivism*.

According to Siemens (2005), connectivism is a combination of theories developed on chaos, networks, and self-organization (p. 7). Connectivism incorporates the following principles:

- Learning and knowledge rests in diversity of opinions.
- Learning is a process of connecting specialized nodes or information sources.
- Learning may reside in non-human appliances.
- Capacity to know more is more critical than what is currently known.
- Nurturing and maintaining connections is needed to facilitate continual learning.
- Ability to see connections between fields, ideas, and concepts is a core skill.
- Currency (accurate, up-to-date knowledge) is the intent of all connectivist learning activities.
- Decision-making is itself a learning process. Choosing what to learn and the meaning of incoming information is seen through the lens of a shifting reality. While there is a right answer now, it may be wrong tomorrow due to alterations in the information climate affecting the decision. (Siemens, 2005, p.7)

A critical part of this learning theory is the role of a network in an individual's learning. Without access to and participation in the organizations that comprise networks or connections between information, an individual's knowledge development would be limited. This concept of networked learning is very similar to Lave and Wenger's legitimate peripheral participation framework (1991). The difference is that Siemens very directly notes that access to these organizations, information, and knowledge happens through technology.

Additionally, a key principle of connectivism that is relevant when considering social media and collaboration tools is that learning is not about memorization or deep understanding of specific topics. Technology makes these cognitive processes obsolete. Instead, learning is about being able to make connections across information that exists outside an individual in order to solve problems. This information can be accessed and interpreted through the Internet, using a variety of web tools and applications.

While constructivism, legitimate peripheral practice, and cognitive apprenticeship all recognize the importance of other individuals and human networks in learning, they do not implicate technology in the process. Connectivism fills this gap and necessitates a closer look at the ways that web applications and tools make connecting easier and more effective for individuals and organizations.

SUMMARY

Social interaction, artifact development, collaboration, cooperation, authenticity, and apprenticeship are important parts of designing social learning experiences. This can be seen in the decades of research supporting fundamental theories behind social learning and learning with technology, such as constructivism, constructionism, and connectivism.

Furthermore, two applications of these learning theories are Lave and Wenger's (1991) framework for legitimate peripheral participation and Collins, Brown, and Newman's (1989) cognitive apprenticeship. These theories and framework together offer a valuable foundation for the study of social learning and the development and integration of relative social media and collaboration-enhancing tools.

Educational concepts such as constructionism, social learning, and legitimate peripheral participation are quickly translating into the forms of "learning to be" that are proposed to replace the traditional Cartesian education model, which looks at learning as a form of transmission of knowledge from teacher to student (Brown & Adler, 2008). The idea of "social learning" is not a new one; theories that suggest learning are participatory; and knowledge is constructed by participants who have been around for quite some time.

Distance learning, virtual reality, collaboration, access to tools via online platforms, and online communities of practice where experts and novices can discuss and learn together are alternatives to traditional brick-and-mortar, lecture-based classroom learning that are already quite popular in K–12, higher education, and even workplace learning situations. This learning is not just a repository of traditional course materials available online, but also the access to experts, resources, and opportunities to participate in "real" discussion. Connectivism demonstrates the growing relevance of technology in learning.

However, despite the growing agreement among educators and researchers that individuals can learn just as well in unstructured, informal social environments through the web as they can in traditional classroom environments, there is still a need for systems, learning environments, and learning activities. These must help individuals sift and filter all of the information out there, understand the history of domains and disciplines and the languages and knowledge they have already built, and learn how to make informed decisions about what to learn and how to learn. Otherwise, we might have a mish-mosh of misinformed, misguided citizens.

In light of this shift, it is imperative that we continue to explore the relevance and importance of established social learning theories and what they have to offer to learning facilitators, teachers, instructional designers, and other educational leaders as they use social media and collaboration tools to support learning in any environment.

DISCUSSION QUESTIONS

1. Compare constructivism and/or constructionism. What are the similarities and differences? When might one more appropriately fit a learning situation than the other?
2. Think of a teaching or learning scenario from your experience (or hypothetical) that demonstrated constructionism. How did constructionism benefit the learners? Who were the learners? What were the learning objectives? What tools or resources made the learning experience a success?
3. Imagine you were asked to design a learning activity for children participating in a reading program at your local library. You must use constructivist theory to inform your design. Explain at least three tasks or steps that comprise the activity and how each element of the activity aligns with social constructivism.
4. How might you design a training for ten new medical interns at a hospital using the concept of legitimate peripheral participation? What learning objectives would be involved? What activities would be necessary? What tools and resources would you need?
5. Cognitive apprenticeship is still frequently used in many professions today. What is an example of a profession where cognitive apprenticeship is used? What would make a successful application of cognitive apprenticeship versus a failed application of cognitive apprenticeship?

6. Taking on a connectivist perspective, list three types of individual cognitive processes that may not be as important or even obsolete when considering what is meant by "learning." Explain why these processes can be "off-loaded" onto technology.
7. Name two specific web apps or tools that might allow new engineers at NASA to start considering the most important issues or problems to solve at the organization in their first year. Why are those apps or tools the best place to start?

REFERENCES

Bers, M. (2001). Identity construction environments: Developing personal and moral values through the design of a virtual city. *The Journal of the Learning Sciences*, *10*(4), 365–415.

Blomenfeld, P. C., & Soloway, E. (1991). Motivating project-based learning: Sustaining the doing, supporting the learning. *Educational Psychologist* 26(3&4): 369–398.

Brown, S., & Adler, R. (2008). Minds on fire. *Educause Review*, pp. 17–32.

Chaiklin, S. (2003). The zone of proximal development in Vygotsky's analysis of learning and instruction. In *Vygotsky's educational theory in cultural context* (pp. 39–64). Cambridge: Cambridge University Press.

Collins, A., Brown, J. S., & Newman, S. E. (1989). Cognitive apprenticeship: Teaching the craft of reading, writing and mathematics. *Thinking: The Journal of Philosophy for Children*, *8*(1), 2–10.

Donovan, M. S., Bransford, J. D., & Pellegrino, J. W. (Eds.). (1999). *How people learn: Bridging research and practice*. Washington, DC: National Academies Press.

Lave, J., & Wenger, E. (1991). *Situated learning: Legitimate peripheral participation*. Cambridge: Cambridge University Press.

Papert, S., & Harel, I. (1991). Situating constructionism. *Constructionism*, *36*, 1–11.

Piaget, J. (1983). Piaget's theory. In P. Mussen (Ed.), *Handbook of child psychology*. New York: Wiley.

Rogoff, B. (1994). Developing understanding of the idea of communities of learners. *Mind, Culture, and Activity*, *1*(4): 209–29.

Schoenfeld, A. H. (1985). *Mathematical problem solving*. New York: Academic Press.

Schon, D. (1987). *Educating the reflective practitioner: Toward a new design for teaching and learning in the professions*. San Francisco, CA: Jossey-Bass Inc.

Siemens, G. (2005). Connectivism: A learning theory for the digital age. *International Journal of Instructional Technology and Distance Learning*, *2*(1), 3–10.

Vygotsky, L. (1978). Interaction between learning and development. *Readings on the Development of Children*, *23*(3), 34–41.

Chapter 3

Social Media Tools and Learning

OBJECTIVES

At the conclusion of this chapter, you will be able to:

1. Define "social media" and analyze its use and purpose in society (ISTE 1).
2. Describe and analyze examples of social media tools (ISTE 1).
3. Distinguish between various social media features and the interactions and benefits they allow users (ISTE 1).
4. Recognize and evaluate strategies to leverage social media tools and their features to facilitate learning and support learners (ISTE 5, 6).
5. Synthesize social learning theory and strategies for using social media tools for learning to develop robust learning experiences (ISTE 5, 6).

EXAMPLES OF SOCIAL MEDIA TOOLS

Social media tools are designed to support social activities, such as meeting new people; staying in touch with family, friends, colleagues, and coworkers; sharing information, and simply being entertained by the goings-on in the daily lives of others, all through the Internet. These communication and networking activities are supported and make up the "social" component of "social media."

Additionally, most of these tools let users share some combination of text, image, video, sound, and links in a cloud-based digital environment, which comprises the "media" aspect of "social media." Thus, "social media" can be defined as a combination of text, image, video, sound, and links that allow individuals to communicate through the Internet.

Popular social media tools of the early twenty-first century include Facebook, Instagram, and LinkedIn. Many of these tools are available for use through short message service (SMS/text), website, and/or mobile app. Each has its own unique interface, but their audience, purpose, and features are very similar.

Facebook was originally developed in 2004 for college students to communicate with each other during and after their studies. At one point, an e-mail address with an .edu domain was required to get a Facebook account. In other words, one needed to be an enrolled learner at a college or university to use the service.

Eventually, Facebook opened up their service to the whole world, and anyone from 0 to 100 years old, regardless of education, could get an account. All that was required was an e-mail address. Users can connect with their friends, post their ideas and images, comment and "like" each other's posts, and create groups and events.

Twitter was created in 2006 shortly after Facebook was launched. Recognizing a need for a simpler social networking solution, Twitter limited communications between its users to 160-character text messages. Twitter eventually allowed users to post or share pictures, gifs, and videos and increased its character count to 280.

Instagram is another social media tool that was created by Facebook, Inc. in 2010. It functions in a very similar way regarding maintaining connections and sharing information. The key difference is that the "media" aspect of Instagram is focused more on image and video than on text and linking. Individuals who enjoy taking photos and videos or who are more visually oriented can easily share their works with their contacts on Instagram.

Snapchat is a mobile app that allows users to create and share photos, video, and text that disappear from both users' phones upon the recipient opening them. Snapchat has colorful and fun photo and video filters, friend emoticons, and other editing options that allow users to create and share their own personalized and customized masterpieces. A unique feature of Snapchat compared to other social media is that users do not see each other's contact lists, so it is not as much for networking as it is for communicating.

YouTube gives users a platform to share videos they have created and comment on other videos. This was one of the first social media sites where Internet users were creating the content rather than the company that created the site creating the content. Users can create their own YouTube channel and subscribe to each other's channels. They can also create watchlists, vote for videos they like or dislike, and embed or link to videos in other sites, such as their personal website or on other social media sites.

LinkedIn is the professional, workplace- and job-oriented answer to Facebook. It was developed to help individuals create a digital resume and conduct digital networking. People promote their professional expertise by listing their experience and education and find job opportunities without leaving home. LinkedIn originally started as a resume-sharing and networking service, but it quickly became a professional and personal news and information sharing service as well.

After the dawn of social media, software developers continued to appeal to users' love of socializing on the Internet. They attempted to create similar sites that had different appearance or targeted different markets. Social media sites such as Pinterest and Ello serve specific markets such as these. There are some developed specifically for education settings and teachers as well.

EdModo is an example of a social media tool developed specifically for education settings. It functions similarly to Facebook, but the access to the product can be kept private to a particular class, school, district, or workplace. The features are more targeted to educators who want to connect with the whole community around the learner. It is also more easily controlled by educators who are concerned for young learners' privacy.

SOCIAL MEDIA FEATURES

In order to explore the teaching and learning strategies and types of activities that can be developed using social media tools, it is important to get a sense of the range of features that social media tools offer. Many tools share the same features; they are often simply organized differently or promoted for various users and uses.

Becoming familiar with the features of each tool, their advantages and disadvantages, and the ways they are organized and presented will help in making a decision as to which tools may best suit the audience and context at hand. Described below are some common features across social media.

- Profile—A public-facing page the user develops with personal information such as name and location as well as photos, videos, and links (see figure 3.1).
  - Advantages: Users can construct their digital identity, personalize their accounts, and find others with similar or unique interests without directly contacting them. This reduces time needed for ice breakers and helps those who are not good at remembering names or socializing in person.
  - Disadvantages: Users may not be clear on how social media companies use their profile data. Photos and videos may be publicly searchable. Users can become targets for unwanted advertising or cyberbullying based on information added to their profile.

- Chat message (individual, group)—Also known as a private message or direct message, a chat message can be sent using a chat box within the tool (see figure 3.2). This allows users to communicate with each other directly while using the tool without making public posts or sending e-mail or text message to an outside service.
  - Advantages: Not all information is suitable for group or public viewing. Users should have an option for private and one-on-one discussions.

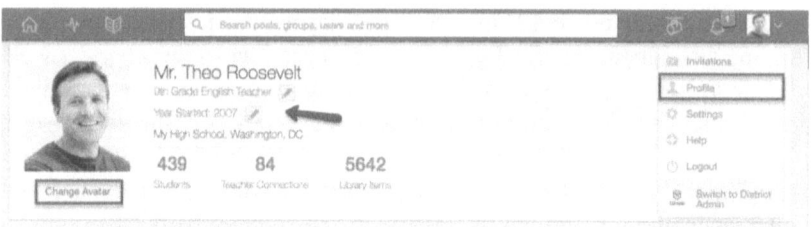

Figure 3.1. Sample Edmodo profile (Edmodo.com, 2017).

Figure 3.2. Google Hangouts chat box.

- Disadvantages: Users may share information privately in a chat message because they are shy, unsure, or do not prefer group communication, which may limit the development of group knowledge. Users may share information in a chat message that may be offensive or inappropriate. A moderator such as a teacher cannot monitor this communication easily.
- E-mail message—Rather than using personal e-mail to communicate with other users, the user can send an e-mail to another user's e-mail address using the system's internal e-mail messaging service. The sender's and recipient's personal e-mail addresses will remain private.
  - Advantages: Users may check their e-mail more frequently than they check messages in an app or tool, so e-mailing from within the system may expedite communication. Many e-mail systems allow users to sort more easily by date, sender, and subject compared to social media tools. Some e-mail systems allow for encryption, which provides more security.
  - Disadvantages: Users may share information privately in an e-mail that would be better shared within the app or tool for record-keeping purposes or for development of group knowledge. Users may share information in a chat message that may be offensive or inappropriate. A moderator such as a teacher cannot monitor this communication easily.
- Text message (individual, group)—Rather than sharing a mobile number to communicate by phone with other users, the user can send a text message to another user's mobile device using the system's internal text messaging service. The sender's and recipient's personal mobile numbers will remain private.
  - Advantages: Users may check their phone for text messages more frequently than they check messages or notifications within an app or tool, so a text from the system may expedite communication or signal urgency of a message.
  - Disadvantages: Text messages from social media apps can seem intrusive if there is no user control to turn this feature on and off. Additionally, some users may not want to provide their mobile number to the social media tool for privacy reasons.
- Individual contacts or connections—One user can add another user to their list of contacts, which in turn allows the users to see each other's information shared through the tool, such as posts, photos, links, other contacts, etc. (see figure 3.3). A contact or connection typically requires "accepting" the other user's invitation to connect by clicking an "Accept" button to confirm mutual agreement about the connection.
  - Advantages: Users can easily build a social network and share information with individuals they choose much more quickly and without as

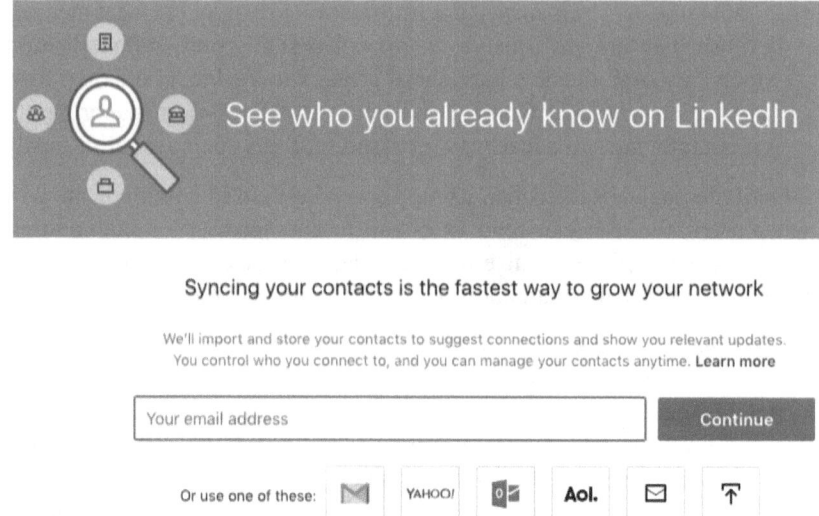

Figure 3.3. Finding contacts on LinkedIn.

much effort as would be required for in-person social settings. Users can review profiles of prospective contacts before accepting the invitation to connect.
- Disadvantages: When a user does not wish to make a connection with someone who has requested one, the rejected or ignored connection may be obvious to the other party.
• Group contacts/connections—A user can be added or add oneself to a group list created by another user. The initiator or leader of the group often must accept or confirm the new user to become part of the group and see other group member's information shared through the tool, such as posts, photos, links, and other contacts.
  - Advantages: Users who may not have connected with others individually through a personal or professional connection can join groups that are of interest to them and have access to the individuals, resources, and knowledge of those groups.
  - Disadvantages: Groups can become too large to manage for certain purposes, so membership may need to be limited. If a group is not monitored appropriately, the conversations can go off-topic or become inappropriate. Irrelevant contributions may be overlooked.
• Import contacts—Many social media tools allow users to import their contact list from their e-mail service or mobile device to help them find contacts that may also be using the service. The tool automatically syncs with

the relevant e-mail or mobile service provider and asks the user for confirmation to make the connection or contact through the tool.

- Advantages: Automating the import of contacts can save time. This process quickly builds the user's network based on previous or existing contacts without much effort.
- Disadvantages: Some contacts may not be appropriate connections depending on the type of social media. For example, a friend may be an appropriate contact on Snapchat but may not be an appropriate contact on LinkedIn. This means users may have to select from their contacts one by one.

• Post or upload of media—Users can publicly share text, audio, video, photo, and links with other users by posting or uploading them to one of several areas on the tool, such as a personal page or group page (see figure 3.4). These pages are often called timelines or feeds. Additionally, the user can usually select whether the post is viewable by the public or by select users of the tool. They can also "tag" the names of other users or groups who may be interested or affiliated with the post's content and also "pin" their location if the post involves a geographic region.

- Advantages: Multimedia and multimodal communication will benefit users who prefer communication including and beyond text. Links and media from other places on the web can help users find additional information that is relevant or useful to them.
- Disadvantages: Users may link to or upload media that is inappropriate, inaccurate, lacks credibility, or is irrelevant to another person, group, or conversation. Individuals who are tagged and places that are pinned may create privacy concerns if one wishes to keep one's identity, affiliation, or location private.

• Reactions and comments—Once users view a post from another user, they can react with an icon such as a thumbs-up, a "like," or a smiley face. They can also reply to the post with text, image, audio, video, or link.

- Advantages: Reactions and comments are a quick and effective way to show support, opinion, or emotion toward a connection, event, or idea. Those who may not have much to say can still share a reaction and observe how others react.
- Disadvantages: Users sometimes use social media tools to make reactions and comments they would not make if they were face-to-face with the individual with whom they are communicating. There can also be a tendency toward "group think" or bullying when posts, reactions, and comments are viewable by large number of people and topics of

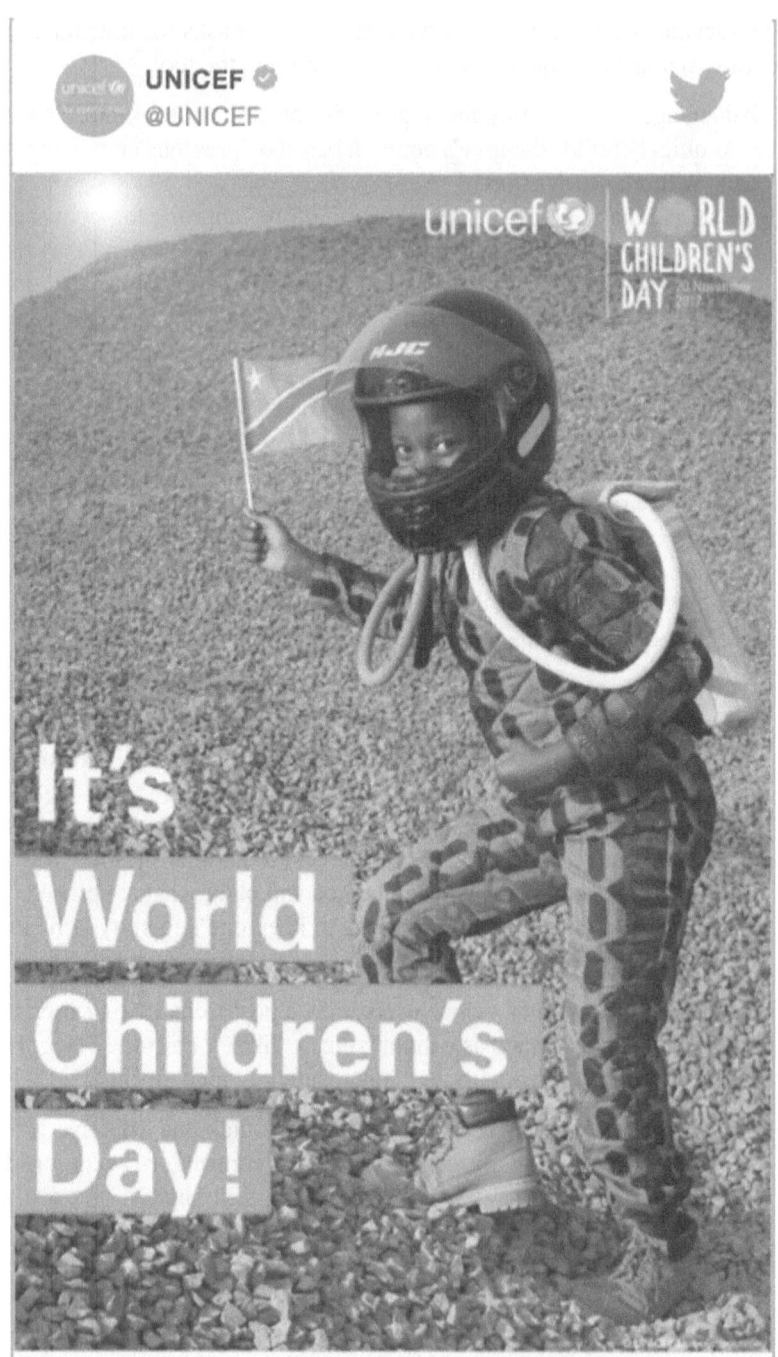

Figure 3.4. Example of a post to Twitter.

conversations are contentious. Additionally, some reactions and comments may come from phony paid users.

- Themed or community content pages—A user can share information about a business, event, or organization by creating a page separate from their personal profile page, such as a group page, event page, or organization page (see figure 3.5). Users can add these pages to their contacts list so that any information shared on those pages appears in their feed along with posts from other individual users. This is also called "Following."

  - Advantages: After following an event or community page, users will find others with similar interests or who attend the same events and grow their network. Additionally, many social media tools will recommend similar events, groups, communities, or artists, which can also help users grow their network and gain new experiences.
  - Disadvantages: The events, groups, communities, or artists that social media tools may recommend to a user may cause them to only connect with individuals who have similar views and interests as their own. This can cause a lack of diversity in experiences, beliefs, and their network as a whole.

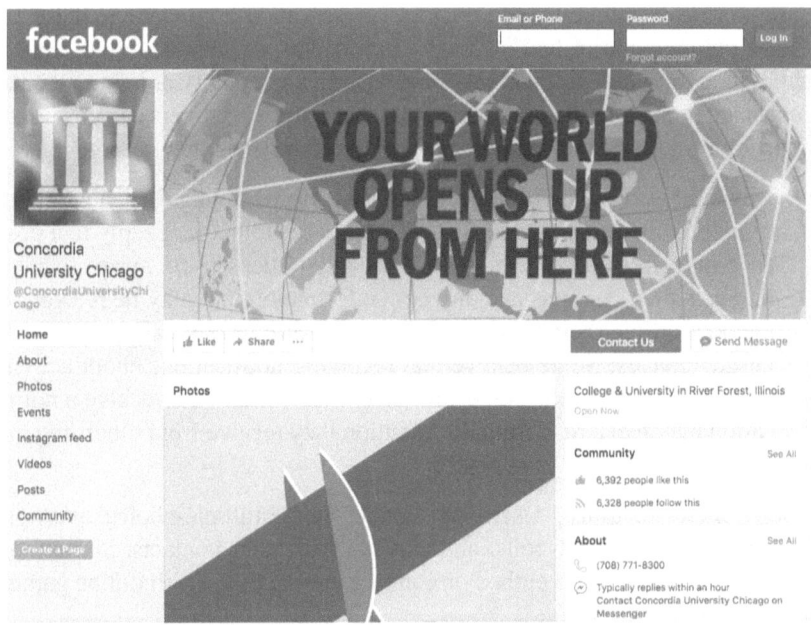

Figure 3.5. Facebook page for Concordia University Chicago.

- Advertising—Many of the social media tools stay profitable by selling ad space on their sites. Users can interact with the ad content by reacting with a like, comment, or share.
  - Advantages: Advertisers may expose users to products or services that will support their interests or otherwise benefit them personally or professionally.
  - Disadvantages: Advertisers often collect data about users from social media companies but users are unaware of the type of data that is collected or the methods used to collect it. Users must read Terms and Conditions carefully when using social media tools.
- Privacy settings—Users can choose whether specific contacts, content, and interactions are viewable or interactable by the public, other users of the tool, or specific contacts.
  - Advantages: Users have control over their interactions and connections. They can share content with different types of contacts without switching systems. If a user is uncomfortable with a connection or with sharing information to a group, they can control those interactions as well.
  - Disadvantages: Privacy settings can become so complex that the user becomes confused about what they are sharing, such as who can view their profile, who knows they are using the tool, or who can see their posts.
- Monitoring interactions with content—Also called notifications, these are some combination of text messages, app badges or sounds, in-tool indications, and/or e-mail notifications when a particular activity or interaction has occurred relative to the user's account (see figure 3.6). Users can customize how much activity information they receive and where they receive it.
  - Advantages: Users will know when they are receiving feedback on one of their interactions on the site (a reaction to an image, a reply to a post, an e-mail from a contact, etc.). This often keeps users aware of what interests their contacts and any new information that may be relevant to them regarding their own contacts, events, or interests.
  - Disadvantages: Some believe that receiving notifications about activity on social media can become addictive. Individuals who receive a notification may feel a rush from the attention they receive from others regarding something they have posted.
- Other included tools—Users can create short multiple-choice questionnaires to elicit voting, polls, and surveys with their contacts. Some tools also include options to embed or connect their activity with online games, stores, and services.
  - Advantages: These extra tools can provide more opportunity for interaction with others, developing knowledge, and growing one's network.

Social Media Tools and Learning

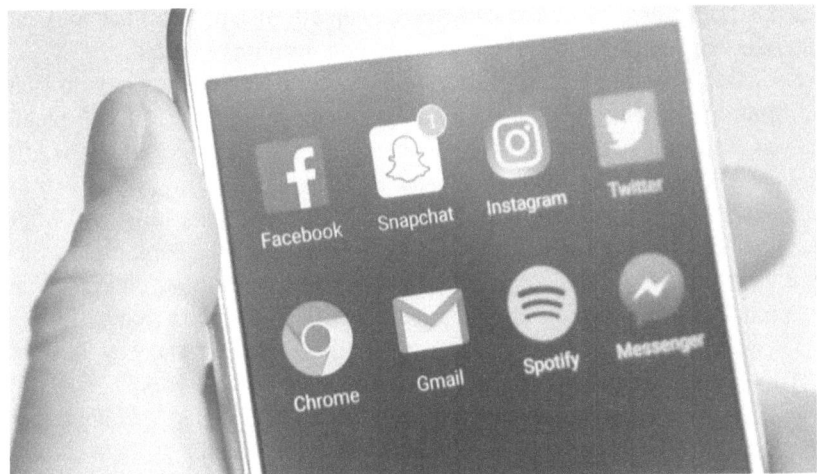

Figure 3.6. Notification from social media app.

- Disadvantages: Not all social media tools offer these additional tools. Some charge a fee for access to full functionality of the additional tools.

These features are just the surface of what social media tools can offer users. Each day, developers are coming up with new ways for users to share and connect. However, the general purpose for social media will likely remain the same so these features will likely stay the same.

Despite all of the advantages of social media, some have said that social media can cause distraction, wasted hours at work, low self-esteem, fear of missing out ("FOMO"), cyberbullying, and stalking. Plus, issues with social media and unreliable sources, fake news, lack of privacy, marketing ploys, and unethical use of data have given it a bad name. As with all technology, there is a dark side and a bright side.

Yet, when it comes to designing learning experiences, the bright side of social media can certainly outweigh the dark. If social media will be used in the classroom, training, or other learning environments, it is critical that those who are initiating its use are aware of the drawbacks and also check with legal and HR departments about potential problems. This is covered in chapter 5.

LEVERAGING SOCIAL MEDIA FEATURES FOR LEARNING

While the value of social media tools for general communication, information sharing, and entertainment is clear, the value of social media tools for learning is not immediately apparent. It may seem as though learners would instinctively communicate with each other through social media forums, but this has not proved to be the case. Established tools such as Facebook and LinkedIn are seen with specific audiences and purposes in mind.

For example, since Facebook started as a site for college learners to share information and network, rather than for academic purposes, it is typically seen as a site for personal use only. There is a similar story with LinkedIn: users see it more for professional and business networking, not for training, academics, or learning. However, of the social media tools that aren't designed specifically for learning, LinkedIn has probably come the farthest relative to offering users more information about continuing education and in-app options for learning through training tools like Lynda.com.

The value of social media tools for learning lies not just in the way they connect individuals who share interests, schools, location, or workplace; having these commonalities does not automatically make for a robust learning experience. Rather, an intentional and planned learning experience along with some form of leadership, apprenticeship, or collaborative goal-setting must take place to elicit a true learning experience with social media tools and their inherent features. The following are some ideas for leveraging the features of social media in order to facilitate the learning process while supporting and motivating learners.

Follow an Expert

Cognitive apprenticeship theory suggests that learners can benefit from exposure to experts and their discourse. Learners who find and follow an expert on social media will receive notifications and be able to view posts, comment, and potentially interact one-on-one with these experts about topics they are learning (see figure 3.7).

For example, a group of learners studying space and flight can be required to follow an astronaut on Twitter or Facebook and share what they are learning by "sharing" the posts from their own accounts.

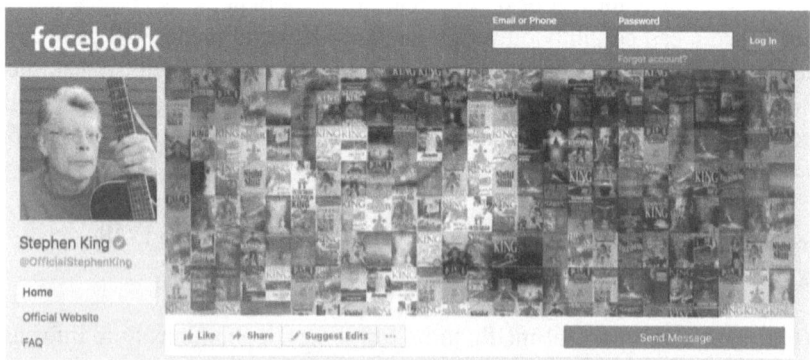

Figure 3.7. Follow an expert such as Stephen King on Facebook.

Join a Group or Organization

One of the key concepts of the legitimate peripheral participation framework is that learning happens through participation in a community of practice. Learners should identify groups and organizations that represent their interests or topics they are learning so as to become more familiar with the community members, language, terms, and any actions or events.

For example, members of an astronomy club might be required to join a Twitter, Facebook, or LinkedIn group such as NASA. Groups such as these often post recent events, news, and opportunities relative to the industry or field, which is an added bonus for those who may be looking to continue their education beyond basic classes and training (see figure 3.8).

Find and Attend an Event

Social media is a free promotion tool for organizations that host events and activities, so learners can find and attend an event that interests them and is related to the topic they are learning, all the while having an authentic experience. This can allow learners to easily find new opportunities while also connecting with others who may or may not be in their network and have similar

Figure 3.8. Join a group or organization such as NASA on Twitter.

interests, which is key for diversifying their experience beyond the classroom or neighborhoods in which they typically interact.

Create an Event, Group, or Themed Page

Besides following individuals and groups and attending events, learners can create their own events, groups, or themed pages around topics they are learning or causes that they support. This opportunity would be a nice follow-up to the more supported activities as those mentioned above, especially when the scaffolds for learning are ready to be removed and learners are okay with moving from the zone of proximal development, exploring ideas, and taking initiative independently.

An example might be a learner who is studying social justice, had a rewarding experience serving the homeless at a soup kitchen, and now wishes to create a volunteer group in her community so others can easily find soup kitchens that need help in the area.

Peer or Leader Recognition

People like gifts and so do learners. Learners can be rewarded by a teacher or trainer who posts a letter of recognition for their good performance or behavior to help motivate and engage them. For example, they may post personal letters of recognition to learners who complete activities accurately and on time. Letters of recognition can easily be done by creating a template stored electronically on word processing software and then simply typing in the learner's name.

Appreciation letters can be tailored to recognized different categories of achievement such as taking extra initiative, creativity and originality, thoroughness, neatness, outstanding work, and significant improvement (see figure 3.9). An image or gif can be posted for a group of learners who won an event.

Administrator Recognition

Never overlook the importance of asking a supervisor or administrator such as a manager, principal, or dean to provide a letter of recognition for a learner's exceptional performance or behavior. Administrators are often viewed highly by learners and to receive verbal recognition or a letter would be motivational.

Leadership and Board Recognition

Like the administrator, teachers can take advantage of the Board of Education by requesting that learners be placed on the agenda at a board meeting so that the learners can be recognized for their outstanding performance. You may allow the learners to provide a description of his or her accomplishment

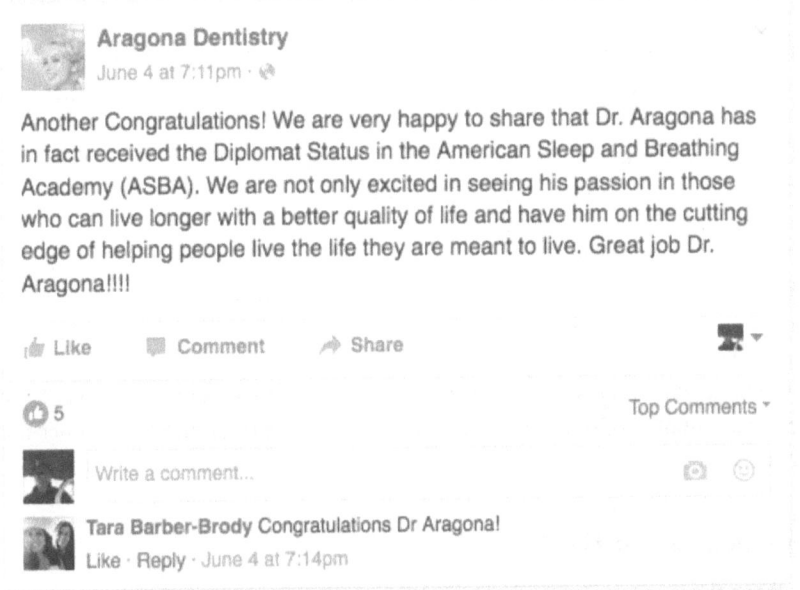

Figure 3.9. Recognition on Facebook (Downs, 2016).

and then allow the board members to ask specific questions. If the learner completed a project, the learner may demonstrate the project to the board members, which can benefit the board members in seeing what some of the results of learners' performance are.

Building Portfolios and Albums of Learning

Learners can also be encouraged to develop a portfolio or album of awards and letters of recognition. The portfolio can act as an incentive to seek more rewards. Certificates of achievements can also be good expressions of appreciation. Certificates can easily be printed on most word processing software. Like letters of appreciation, categories of achievement can also be created such as certificate of academic excellence, attendance, good behavior, best attitude, teamwork, and exceptional effort.

Contests

Contests can be hosted on social media where a leader posts a question to a forum or timeline and the learners who quickly respond with the correct answer in a comment or in a poll can be rewarded with a certificate or token to add to their timeline, portfolio, or album. Those who win the contests can then be the "host" for the next contest, and it can continue on through the whole group or class.

Free stuff

Many retail vendors and nonprofit organizations will offer free merchandise or products for educational purposes and will gladly mention it on their social media pages, especially if it means they will get exposure to an entire network of people who may be interested in their products. A learner or team of learners who achieve good performance could be rewarded with a free pass to a social event or business establishment.

For example, it is common for local businesses such as pizza stores to offer free tokens than can be used for receipt of free or low-cost pizza as a reward for educational or training activities. A common idea is to reward the learner upon reading so many hours or a specific number of books. A special learner might also accompany a teacher to a workshop or to a local sports event. The personal attention can be very motivating for the learner and the teacher may gain a lot of satisfaction as well.

Appreciation Posts

Perhaps there is not a more powerful or popular technique as verbal appreciation. And, this can be accomplished on social media, as well. Teachers and trainers have long recognized the importance of providing positive verbal reinforcement for learners. The simple use of verbal appreciation when presented in a meaningful way can be more powerful than a tangible reward.

For example, there are many expressions that can be used to motivate a learner. One of the more powerful expressions can simply be the statement posted recognizing the entire class for good work.

Surveys

An interesting technique to help learners better understand the cultural beliefs and interests of those inside and outside of their network is with surveys. The survey might consist of a series of questions that ask the learners to rank order items or place their opinions on a Likert scale. Once the survey, used on a social media site, is administered, he or she could compile the results and then develop actions to help address the learners directly through a post or link to the results.

Special Events and Guest Speakers

Hosting special events at a school or using guest speakers to enrich the classroom can break the doldrums of the traditional classroom. A teacher could use social media to broadcast to the community about a special topic.

For example, a science teacher bringing in an orthopedic surgeon and demonstrating how to repair a broken leg by putting a cast on a learner's leg can be very enriching. The surgeon could explain the concept of a fracture and then actually put a cast on a learner's leg and then allow the learners to all sign their autograph on the cast. At the completion of the exercise the surgeon could then demonstrate the removal of the cast by cutting the cast off and then allowing the learner to keep the cast as a souvenir.

SUMMARY

Social media tools have come a long way since they were first developed. They have many useful features that align with established social learning theories and can be leveraged for learning environments.

The variety of tools out there can make it a little overwhelming to choose the one that makes sense for a particular activity. Facebook, Instagram, Snapchat, and LinkedIn were some of the first of hundreds of social media tools that have come and gone. They are evidence of the importance of users' desire to connect with each other and share information and media in a simple and user-friendly manner. They were not initially created for educational purposes, so it is important to choose carefully.

Many of the social media have similar features. If an activity doesn't work using one type of social media tool, trying with another will not be too time-intensive or create too much of a learning curve on the technical end. However, it is best to get a sense for which ones will meet your learners' needs across multiple activities before making a decision and implementing those related activities.

Activities that can be successful on social media include following an expert, leading a discussion, or sharing media on a topic. Public recognition is another easy win for learners through social media, though not a learning activity in itself. Learners can also create their own content and community pages on social media, which will create a sense of ownership and authenticity unmatched by more structured, instructor-led activities. Social media is only limited by the creativity and imagination of its users.

DISCUSSION QUESTIONS

1. A group of high school students are studying modern art and a field trip to the local Modern Arts Museum is planned this month. What type of social media strategies could the teacher implement to help the learners have a more robust interaction? Why are these strategies best for this learner group and setting?

2. A large fast-food restaurant chain wants to help their new trainees from different locations across town get to know each other while also creating a little competition among them. What are some social media features and strategies that the trainer could use to accomplish this objective? Describe a step-by-step activity that the trainer would follow.
3. A nonprofit organization that provides food and clothing for the homeless is trying to get more volunteers in the door to be trained and serve at their distribution centers. How might the organization use social media tools to educate the public about their needs and potentially gain more support? Explain the rationale for the social media tools and activities chosen.

EXERCISES

Developing an Instructional Design That Uses Social Media Tools
Directions: Complete the following worksheet to plan for an instructional session that uses at least one social media tool described in this chapter.

Session Title: _____   Date: _____
Facilitator: _____   Participants: _____

Planning

1. Write your objective(s): At the conclusion of the session, the participants will be able to:

_____
_____
_____
_____
_____

2. Select the domain(s) of learning (affective, cognitive, psychomotor):

_____
_____
_____
_____
_____

3. List the instructional methods and/or theories applied:

_____
_____
_____
_____

4. Write the level of taxonomy of objectives (refer to chapter 1):

_____
_____
_____
_____

5. List the instructional materials, supplies, and tools, including social media tools:

_____
_____
_____
_____

Opening

6. Write an opening statement (or outline):

_____
_____
_____
_____
_____

Facilitating and instructing

7. Write an outline for your session, including any scaffolds and activities (independent or group):

Topic 1: _____
Subtopic: _____
Subtopic: _____
Activity _____
(Transition): _____

Topic 2: _____
Subtopic: _____
Subtopic: _____
Activity _____
(Transition): _____

Topic 3: _____
Subtopic: _____
Subtopic: _____
Activity: _____
(Transition): _____

8. List methods to engage and keep your participants motivated:

_____
_____
_____
_____
_____

Closing and assessing

9. Write a summary or closing statement of the learning experience:

10. List the methods of assessment:

11. List any documentation or follow-up needed:

REFERENCES

Downs, T. (2016, November 01). Social media for dentists done right: 4 things you can do this week. Retrieved March 15, 2018, from https://titanwebagency.com/blog/dentistry-social-media/.

Edmodo.com (2017). Set up your teacher profile (Teacher). Edmodo.com. Retrieved March 15, 2018, from https://support.edmodo.com/hc/en-us/articles/205009164-Set-Up-Your-Teacher-Profile-Teacher.

Chapter 4

Collaboration Tools and Learning

OBJECTIVES

At the conclusion of this chapter, you will be able to:

1. Describe and analyze examples of collaboration tools (ISTE 1).
2. Distinguish between various collaborative tools features and the interactions and benefits they allow users (ISTE 1).
4. Recognize and evaluate strategies to leverage collaboration tools and their features to facilitate learning and support learners (ISTE 4, 5).
5. Synthesize social learning theory and strategies for using collaboration tools to develop robust learning experiences (ISTE 4, 5, 6).

WHAT IS A COLLABORATION TOOL?

Before the Internet connected the world, collaboration almost always occurred in person. People would share words, ideas, drawings, gestures, artifacts, files, and writing in conference rooms, classrooms, study halls, libraries, or home offices.

Collaboration is often defined as communication between two or more people to reach a specific goal. There are many tools that support collaboration. Basic collaboration tools include a conference phone that allows individuals to discuss an idea, a whiteboard where individuals can write out their ideas so all can see, or even a shared file folder on a company network that lets employees share files with each other. Items such as sticky notes, flipcharts, and projected presentations are additional tools that are often considered useful for collaboration.

While it has always been possible to visit someone in person, call someone, or send a document through postal mail to collaborate, there are several limitations to these non-digital, non-virtual forms of collaboration. The amount of time to reach a goal and the confusion that may ensue when more than two people needed to collaborate on one task can become very difficult.

For example, having four people on a conference phone line trying to learn how to complete a task with a new software application would become difficult for a few reasons:

1. There is no way to share visual information without having to describe it verbally in detail while only using a phone. This would take much longer than sharing the visual information in person, such as sitting next to someone on a computer.
2. It is difficult to distinguish who is speaking when four people are on a conference line, especially if they are not familiar with each other's voices.
3. Many of the nonverbal cues used in group conversations that help people know when to start and stop talking (or listening) are missing.

Digital tools for communication now make collaboration between multiple individuals possible over the Internet, a phone line, or through an organization's internal computer network. As with anything digital, these tools provide a more convenient alternative to meeting in person for people who live in different geographic regions or who otherwise cannot meet in the same time and place for any reason. Collaboration tools discussed from this point forward will be only those that are digital.

EXAMPLES OF COLLABORATION TOOLS FOR LEARNING

A wide range of virtual collaboration tools is available as cloud- and web-based applications or for download onto a personal computer or mobile phone (see figure 4.1). Some tools are designed for a mainstream or general public audience to use how they wish. Others are designed specifically with a professional or workplace audience in mind. Many tools for collaboration are free to use with options to purchase additional features and services. All that is needed is an Internet connection.

Skype is an app that uses Voice Over Internet Protocol (VOIP) technology to allow individuals to conduct video and voice calls over the Internet between devices such as cellular phones and laptops. Skype also allows for calls to be made to standard telephone lines, lets users chat with text, and provides a space for exchange of files and documents. For example, after being

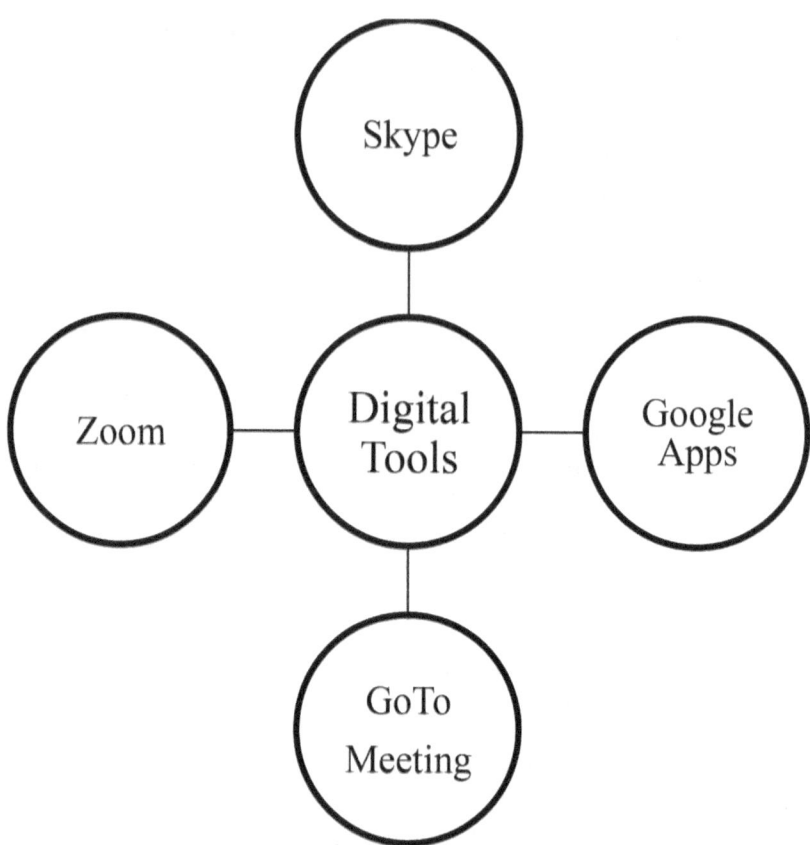

Figure 4.1. Examples of collaborative digital tools.

assigned to a group project, learners talk with each other on Skype over the weekend to discuss who will take on specific responsibilities for a project.

- Advantages: Skype is well-known internationally and has a simple interface. Users do not have to share their e-mail address or phone number with other users to communicate. Skype users can talk to other Skype users for free.
- Disadvantages: Users who call land lines or mobile phone numbers from Skype pay a fee. The limit on number of users on a Skype call is 25, sometimes less for video calls.

Google offers a suite of apps that gives users several options for collaboration over the Internet. Users can share files and folders and edit documents, spreadsheets, and presentations together in real time. While they are editing, they can also use text chat or video call tools within the suite to talk with

Collaboration Tools and Learning 59

each other and set up appointments that are linked to their Google calendar or e-mail apps. A local organization that is collaborating on an upcoming presentation might employ collaboration apps such as Google Slides to create the slideshow together, Google Hangouts to see and talk to each other (see figure 4.2), and Google Calendar to set up future meeting dates.

- Advantages: Google has real-time, in-document collaboration capability. Google's app interoperability for users with a Google account is what initially sets Google's apps apart from many other collaboration tools. Users do not have to login to other accounts to use the apps they need.
- Disadvantages: Google collects data on all interactions in their apps. If users are only using Google products for all of their needs, privacy and security of data stored in Google apps could be a concern. Google also has been fairly slow to increase the features and affordances of their apps, so they are as sophisticated and robust as some of their competitors.

In the professional and workplace sector, many organizations use collaboration tools such as GoToMeeting and Zoom. Unlike Skype and Google apps, these tools are designed specifically for hosting virtual workplace meetings that may have several attendees. Similar to Skype and Google apps, they allow voice calls, webcam and screen sharing, text chat, and file sharing. They also have features that support common workplace tasks such as presentation mode, breakout groups, polling, and voting. Virtual teams across locations who need to meet for large- and small-group work would benefit from this type of collaboration tool.

- Advantages: These tools have a wide variety of features that support almost any type of work-related communication task. Users have many more

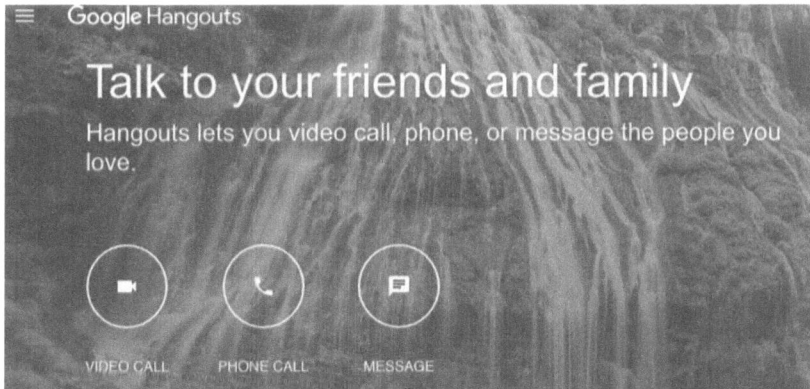

Figure 4.2.   Google Hangouts interface.

options for how they and their audience can see and interact with the tool's interface.
- Disadvantages: Users may need to be trained in how to use some of the more advanced features of these tools. Audience members who are not regular users may not see the tool as intuitive and could become frustrated. Some may feel the additional features are too distracting or complex.

Taking a more visual approach to collaboration, RealtimeBoard is a tool that lets users focus on development of visual artifacts such as concept maps, presentations, and mockups. Features such as virtual sticky notes and multicolored freehand drawing tools give users an experience similar to using a real-life whiteboard (see figure 4.3). The tool also offers presentation mode, screen sharing, and real-time editing. Students in a high school architecture class could share their ideas for a building design without having to move seats or meet in person.

- Advantages: Visual editing features are extremely useful for users whose work tasks are very visual or require a lot of space to share drawings, illustrations, or concept maps. The interface can be engaging and exciting since there are additional tools to explore beyond those of basic collaboration tools.

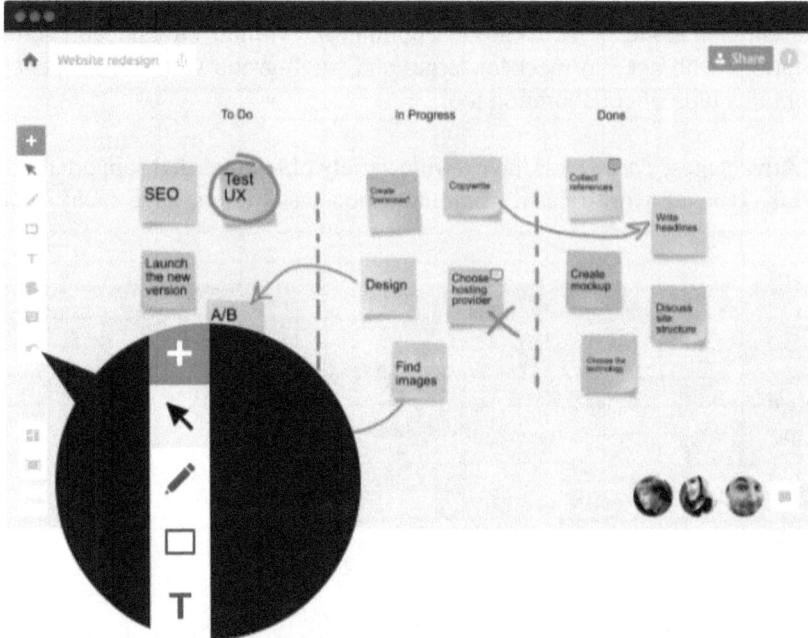

Figure 4.3. Whiteboard feature on RealtimeBoard.

- Disadvantages: Like some of the advanced meeting tools for collaboration, users may need to be trained in how to use some of the more advanced features of these visually oriented tools. Audience members who are not regular users may not see the tool as intuitive and could become frustrated. Some may feel the additional features are too distracting, complex, or unnecessary.

Wikipedia is an example of another type of collaboration tool that lets collaborators add and edit text, images, and video on a series of web pages simply by logging in to a website. This type of tool is what is known as a "wiki." At its root, a wiki is simply a database of websites that users access virtually. Depending on the permission level, the user can make a limited set of changes with simple text editors and see the changes other users have made as well. College professors have had their students contribute information and research to public wikis on specific topics to generate knowledge among people outside of their school.

- Advantages: Contributing to a public wiki is an authentic publishing task. The content a user or group of users adds will be viewable to the world. It can empower learners and help them recognize the ways knowledge is situated and constructed socially.
- Disadvantages: The interface and navigation of wikis can be very basic, which can make users and viewers lose interest. Also, since many wikis are public, users need to be careful when they add or share information, so they do not violate their organization's policies. They also need to monitor their content since others can edit it without their permission.

Slack is an example of an application that collaborators can use to send group messages and direct messages, make voice calls, and share files with each other. The interface is similar to a virtual chat room, with separate conversations and threads streaming down the page vertically. There are also options to create different channels that users can subscribe to or be invited to if there is a need for discussions around different topics (see figure 4.4). It is a simple way to communicate but also document and manage knowledge across an organization. Slack is used by employees, gamers, students, and virtually any type of virtual team to keep in touch and share information.

- Advantages: The interface is fun and engaging. There are many social media–style features such as channels and direct messaging. The features are simple and easy to learn to use.
- Disadvantages: Users will have to login to another collaboration tool to manage projects and to develop documents and other artifacts together.

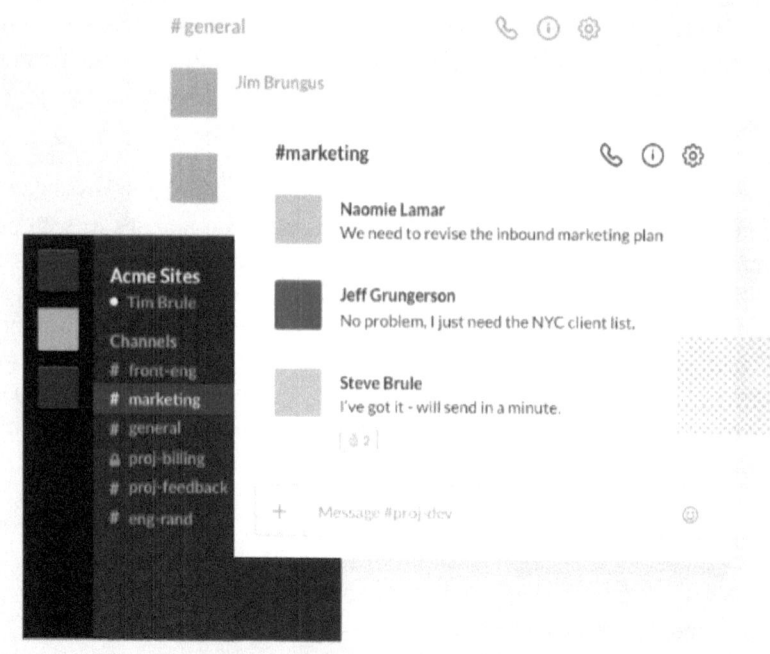

Figure 4.4. Channels and group messages in Slack.

For those who wish to manage projects and communicate about them in a collaborative fashion, Trello is a growingly popular application. Users are presented with a project board, which is a visual display of information about projects, what stage they are at, and which users are working on them. Comments, labels, and checklists are used to keep all users on track and discussing where they are at on specific topics for any given project. A drag-and-drop feature, as well as clear dropdown menus and intuitive button options, makes this type of software very helpful for visual learners and those who do not have time to learn more sophisticated project management software.

- Advantages: Especially useful for workplace and professional settings, this tool allows for communication about completion of tasks in one place so all users can stay on task.
- Disadvantages: This tool may require some training for more advanced features. Users will have to login to another collaboration tool for enhanced communication features and to develop documents and other artifacts together.

Finally, organizations or companies often set up intranets with internal collaboration software such as Microsoft Sharepoint. This type of software allows employees and other members of a specific organization to share, edit, and track files and content. This process is important for knowledge management in companies and is one of the safest tools for collaboration since it happens within the organization and is less likely to be viewed or hacked by external parties, if the organization has a firewall. Organizations can set up folders and websites for each of their departments, so they can quickly share information with each other.

- Advantages: Users have a lot of freedom in how they manage and share their files and other data with this tool. There are many roles, permission levels, and other settings that allow organizations to customize the tool to suit their collaboration and sharing needs.
- Disadvantages: These tools can be expensive. There are also many advanced features and some expertise is required to set up an effective and efficient system. Novice users will need to be trained to use the tool effectively. Use cases may differ across an organization, so different types of training on how to use the tool may be needed.

Many of these tools were initially designed for use in the workplace or for use by the average adult computer user or mobile phone user. However, many learning facilitators and teachers have discovered their use for training, learning, and development purposes; namely, they have made use of the communication, sharing, and information management features of collaboration tools that support the learning process while simultaneously helping learners be productive together and supportive of each other.

COLLABORATION TOOL FEATURES

The range of features that collaboration tools offer for communication, knowledge sharing, and cooperative work is wide. While many share the same features, certain tools may be more advanced in their features than others. Becoming familiar with the features of each tool and the ways they are organized and presented will help in making a decision as to which tools may best suit the audience and context at hand (see figure 4.5).

Digital collaboration tools now allow for communication either synchronously or asynchronously. Synchronous is communication between two or more individuals in real time, such as through a phone call or video stream. Asynchronous is communication between two or more individuals at different times, such as through an e-mail exchange. Each type has its benefits. For

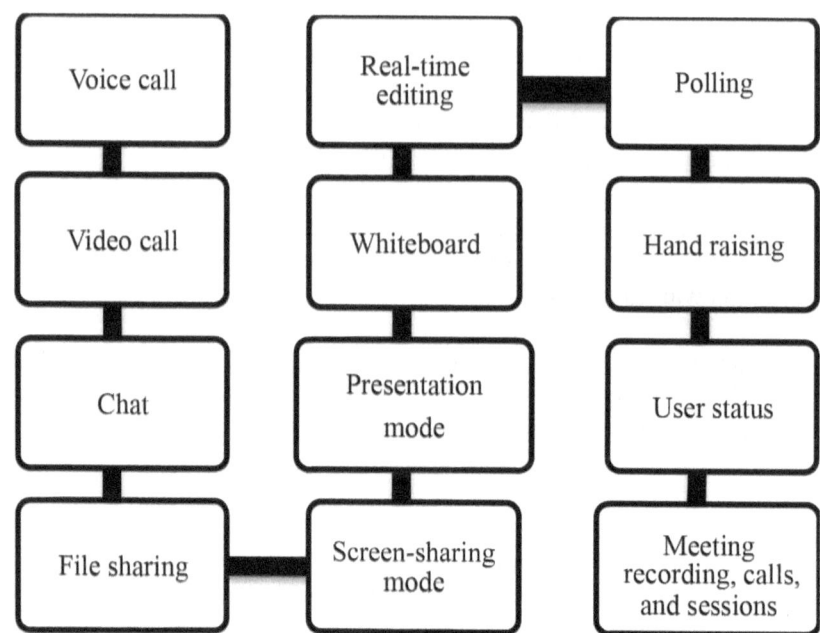

Figure 4.5. Examples of collaborative digital tool features.

example, synchronous communication may be better than asynchronous for brainstorming several ideas quickly since individuals are not waiting for each other to read and respond.

The affordances that a collaboration tool provides for users are just as important as whether the tool has synchronous or asynchronous options. The workplace was the original context for many digital collaboration tools, so many of them took on features that were physically or metaphorically present in the workplace. Below are some key features of digital collaboration tools that allow for effective and efficient collaboration.

- Voice call—With their device's microphone and speakers, collaborators can talk to each other in real time over the Internet. Some tools also offer the option of using a conference call number that allows collaborators who do not have Internet access to still participate in the virtual call.
- Video call—In addition to hearing each other, collaborators can see each other using their device's webcam. This feature is often optional since video can cause connectivity issues if the Internet connection is not strong. The default then is voice only.
- Chat—Collaborators can type messages to each other in a chat box. There is often a choice between large-group chat boxes, where all collaborators can see each other's messages, and private chat boxes between select

collaborators. Chat boxes usually have features that allow users to send live links, as well as images and emoticons.
- File sharing—Rather than e-mailing a file, collaborators can click a share button to link to the file within the app, attach it to a chat message, or drop it in a central virtual drop box for others to view or download.
- Real-time editing—When creating a digital document, spreadsheet, presentation, or other type of file, collaborators can all view and edit the file at the same time. Any modifications are visible to all users.
- Whiteboard—Collaborators can draw pictures, write words, and create flow charts as they would on a real-life whiteboard. This feature typically also allows the user to draw or write freehand or use premade templates, shapes, and other visual objects.
- Presentation mode—A user can configure the screen of the app so that the contents of a slideshow or other artifact are enlarged and take up the most space on the screen so others can easily view it. Other features of the app are still available, though they are likely not as prominently displayed on the screen.
- Screen-sharing mode—When a collaborator has something on his or her computer screen to share with another collaborator, he or she can turn on screen-sharing mode in the app to allow the other collaborators to see it. The screen sharing can be stopped as needed to return back to the main screen.
- Polling—A collaborator can create a virtual poll to get the group's opinion or make decisions.
- Hand Raising—Often used during presentation mode, a collaborator can click a button that presents a visual cue on screen to let a presenter or other collaborators know that he or she has a question.
- User Status—A collaborator can communicate to others that he or she is present, not available, or temporarily away from the meeting or collaboration session by clicking on a button. An on-screen indicator icon, usually next to the name of the user, will let others know of this status without interrupting or requiring further text or voice communication.
- Meeting recording—Many collaboration tools have an option to record the audio and visual content of a session or meeting for individuals who cannot attend or who wish to refer back to something from the meeting at a later time.
- Calls, meetings, sessions, and rooms—Similar to the physical experience of collaboration, collaboration using virtual tools is organized among users through invitations or "joining" virtual calls, virtual meetings or sessions, and/or virtual meeting rooms. A user is invited to participate in a collaborative experience in at least one of these modalities or forums. Some tools also offer additional Group Breakout Rooms embedded within larger calls, meetings, or large-group rooms.

LEVERAGING COLLABORATION TOOLS FOR LEARNING

Almost any project or task can benefit from the wide array of features that today's collaboration tools have to offer. When it comes to learning processes, especially those associated with collaborative and social learning, the possibilities are equally vast.

Even if the learners are in the same location and do not need to communicate virtually, the use of virtual collaboration tools can help learners keep their work organized and communicate more efficiently and effectively. Some tools may also help learners think outside of the box when it comes to managing projects, creating artifacts, and even how to work collaboratively (see figure 4.6).

Below are some examples of learning activities and strategies that can facilitate the social learning process and support collaboration, no matter if the learners are in the same space or not.

Brainstorming

Learners who have been given a new task but are not sure how to carry it out can use features such as file sharing, whiteboard, text chat, voice call, and

Figure 4.6. **Examples of social media learning activities.**

screen sharing to communicate their ideas with each other. It is very easy for multiple users to create an idea board or concept map using many of these tools. Even if only voice, video, and text chat are available with one tool, another tool that does offer those visual tools, such as a virtual whiteboard, can be used at the same time.

Delegating Responsibilities and Outlining Projects

Groups or teams of learners are often given a task but must determine their own specific roles and responsibilities to carry it out. Collaboration tools offer a convenient space for this discussion to happen.

Learners can share their understanding of the tasks involved with a project and associated responsibilities to ensure they are all in agreement. Following that, they can use a shared chart document or whiteboard while simultaneously conducting a voice call to outline a project. Alternatively, they can use a project management tool that helps them collaborate to organize these aspects of a project in a more visual way.

Drafting and Editing

If learners need to create, modify, and/or update a word processing file, spreadsheet, presentation slides, or any other kind of digital artifact, they can use the file-sharing feature and real-time editing feature available in some collaboration software. Learners can also use voice, screen-sharing, and chat features if they prefer to discuss the decisions they are making in real time.

Team Games and Competitions

When groups of learners cannot be in the same room but are interested in some friendly competition, collaboration tools such as whiteboards, shared presentation slides, and voice-only conference calls can be used instead. Breakout rooms and files shared with select users can also allow learners to work collaboratively without the other team hearing or seeing.

Peer Review

Oftentimes teachers and managers require learners to share their work with each other before formally submitting a project. Learners can set up a time and date to discuss each other's work using voice, video, or chat or simply share and comment on files using file-sharing, commenting, and editing features. Software that has recording or documentation of this interaction is extremely helpful for later reference as well.

Information Sharing and Group Discussion

The most standard and popular use of collaboration tools is for sharing information and conducting large-group follow-up discussions of that information. Webinars, virtual meetings, and virtual presentations are the common formats for information sharing and group discussion, using a combination of presentation mode; file sharing; whiteboards; and any type of voice, video, or text communication.

PERSPECTIVES ON COLLABORATION TOOLS FOR LEARNING

Strategies for planning and designing collaborative learning activities in face-to-face and online settings for learners, including those that are technology-supported, has been well-documented (Jonassen, 1999; O'Donnell & Dansereau, 1992; Palincsar & Herrenkohl, 2002). These strategies encourage productive co-regulation, argumentation, and problem solving (Dillenbourg & Tchounikine, 2007; Palincsar & Herrenkohl, 2002). Furthermore, no matter the age of the learner, they will encounter collaborative projects or experiences at some point in their life and should be prepared.

Many argue that there is a difference between group work and true collaboration (Scheuermann, 2018). Group work can simply involve breaking a large project into a series of individual tasks that individuals complete on their own time and in their own space only to put it together with other individual pieces into a final artifact. This can all happen without any collaboration. It is imperative that learning facilitators and teachers keep in mind that strategies for successful collaboration, such as those in table 4.1 and described in the text that follows, must be incorporated alongside the project or learning experience itself.

One strategy for successful collaboration is having learners complete a collaboration plan before they begin working together. This plan would include an outline of the roles and responsibilities required to complete the project.

Table 4.1. Strategies for Successful Collaboration

Collaboration Plan	*Communication Plan*
• Roles and responsibilities	• Preferred methods and modes
• Tasks and steps	• Guidelines and agendas
• Deadlines	• Frequency
• Checkpoints and milestones	• Response time
• Revisit plan and update	• Revisit plan and update

The learners would self-assign these roles and responsibilities or be assigned them by a leader, teacher, or facilitator.

The collaboration plan would also include a list of project components, tasks, or steps required for each component or responsibility, milestones, check-in points, and deadlines. Learners would also list any resources such as files, reports, books, websites, experts, or technology they would need to complete the project. It is best if this plan is completed by all who are collaborating at the start. It should then be followed by a review and revise session at some point during the collaboration to see if anything has changed.

A collaboration communication plan is also useful. Many people begin working on teams assuming that their way of communicating is common or easily adapted by others in the group. Then they find that their group is not meeting deadlines; they begin to resent group members who are not replying to e-mails or seem to be procrastinating. Discussing and establishing expectations and rules for communicating at the beginning of the project is key.

A communication plan should include all collaborators' preferences for communication. For example, some people prefer to talk synchronously only when clarity is needed or a big decision needs to be discussed. Otherwise, they feel that asynchronous group chat messages or e-mail is best since there is a record of participation and decisions. Setting some guidelines like these for the modality for communication is the best place to start. Then, learners can decide on communication aspects such as frequency of discussions, expected response times from collaborators, and the most effective collaboration tools for the task or project at hand.

Furthermore, giving a group of learners or employees access to collaboration tools does not automatically mean collaboration will happen. The learning experience or activity must be designed so that collaboration is possible. Creating challenging projects that are scaffolded with multiple tasks and milestones is a good first step. Learners will quickly realize that they can accomplish the goal much quicker and more effectively if the project is done collaboratively since they can assign tasks across collaborators and share milestones with each other.

Collaborative projects or tasks should also involve a fairly substantial amount of information gathering, problem solving, and decision making. It should also be clear on collaborative projects that innovation and creativity are valued, and that these are often the product of many individuals working together, not just one. In cases where collaborators need to produce a final product, there should be a very specific space or time for this product to be shared, publicly acknowledged, and/or clearly contributing to another purpose. Otherwise, collaborators will not take the project or task seriously and may not hold each other accountable.

In any collaborative project, it is very important for learners to understand the value of collaboration. They should set expectations for communication while collaborating, review best practices for collaborating, and take time to explore the features and technical aspects of collaboration tools.

SUMMARY

The best virtual collaboration tools reflect the best features of the physical classroom and workplace. Whether to simply talk to someone else about their ideas or to demonstrate a particular concept that will be important to complete a project, these tools are becoming more and more popular for collaboration across the world. The benefit of collaboration tools is that learners do not need to be in the same place or even working at the same time. They give learners the opportunity to use them synchronously or asynchronously.

Virtual collaboration tools such as Skype, Google Apps, GoToMeeting, and Sharepoint all have similar communication and sharing features. They all have a text-messaging or voice-call feature that allows users to communicate with each other and share digital information directly as long as they have an Internet connection. There are many collaboration tools that are free. Those that are fee-based often have more sophisticated features and functionality.

Additional features of these tools give groups and teams the opportunity to share files, simultaneously edit documents, create project management boards, illustrate ideas, and collaborate on the creation of artifacts such as reports and spreadsheet. Other useful functionality includes the ability to automatically record or document information shared during a meeting or project session.

Many of the collaborative learning activities and experiences that traditionally happen in person can now happen virtually. Learning tasks such as brainstorming, peer review, and drafting are conducted just as if they were occurring in person—if not more effectively and efficiently. Learners are often given additional tools that can enhance or augment the collaborative experience.

As with any learning experience, it is critical to maintain awareness of the ultimate goal and purpose of the activity. Unfortunately, these collaboration tools do not teach learners how to be good collaborators. In this case, if collaboration is the objective, teachers and facilitators must help learners recognize best practices of collaboration as they are using the tools. Setting up opportunities for activities such as the creation of a collaboration plan or a communication plan is a good start to helping learners maximize the potential of these collaboration tools.

Technology can sometimes hinder a learning process or drive it in a direction that does not necessarily support the original learning objective. It is up to the learning facilitators to maximize the potential of the tools while ensuring that collaboration is ultimately occurring. The tools can only be as productive for collaboration as the collaborators who use them.

DISCUSSION QUESTIONS

1. A group of third-grade students are learning about butterfly life cycle and will be visiting a butterfly conservatory this month. What type of collaborative project might the teacher implement to help the learners make connections between what they are learning in the classroom with what they will see at the conservatory? Why collaborative tools and features might be best for the collaborative project, considering this learner group and setting?
2. A big-box retailer wants to help its new trainees learn about customer service best practices while also creating a little competition among them. What are some collaboration tool features and strategies that the trainer could use to accomplish this objective? Describe a step-by-step activity that the trainer would follow.
3. The director for a national nonprofit organization has new annual fundraising goals she wishes to share with her branch supervisors across the United States. How might she use collaboration tools to carry out this goal while also giving the supervisors opportunities to interact and decide how they will proceed in reaching those goals? Explain the rationale for the collaboration tools and activities chosen.

EXERCISES

Developing an Instructional Design That Uses Collaboration Tools

Directions: Complete the following worksheet to plan for an instructional session that uses at least one collaboration tool described in this chapter.

Session Title: _____ Date: _____
Facilitator: _____ Participants: _____

Planning

1. Write your objective(s): At the conclusion of the session, the participating will be able to:

_____
_____
_____
_____

2. Select the domain(s) of learning:

___

3. List the instructional methods and/or theories applied:

___

4. Write the level of taxonomy of objectives:

___

5. List the instructional materials, supplies, and tools, including collaboration tools:

___

Opening

6. Write an opening statement (or outline):

___

Facilitating and instructing

7. Write an outline for your session, including any scaffolds and activities (independent or group):

Topic 1: _____
Subtopic: _____
Subtopic: _____
Activity: _____
(Transition): _____

Topic 2: _____
Subtopic: _____
Subtopic: _____
Activity: _____
(Transition): _____

Topic 3: _____
Subtopic: _____
Subtopic: _____
Activity: _____
(Transition): _____

8. List methods to engage and keep your participants motivated:

_____
_____
_____
_____

Closing and assessing

9. Write a summary or closing statement of the learning experience:

_____

_____

_____

_____

10. List the methods of assessment:

_____

_____

_____

_____

11. List any documentation or follow-up needed:

_____

_____

_____

_____

REFERENCES

Dillenbourg, P., & Tchounikine, P. (2007). Flexibility in macro-scripts for computer-supported collaborative learning. *Journal of Computer Assisted Learning*, *23*(1), 1–13.

Jonassen, D. H. (1999). Designing constructivist learning environments. In C. M. Reigeluth (Ed.), *Instructional-design theories and models: A new paradigm of instructional theory* (Vol. II, pp. 215–39). Mahwah, NJ: Lawrence Erlbaum Associates.

O'Donnell, A. M. & Dansereau, D. F. (1992). Scripted cooperation in student dyads: A method for analyzing and enhancing academic learning and performances. In R. Hertz-Lazarowitz & N. Miller (ed.), *Interactions in cooperative groups: the theoretical anatomy of group learning* (pp. 120–141). Cambridge: Cambridge University Press.

Palincsar, A. S., & Herrenkohl, L. R. (2002). Designing collaborative learning contexts. *Theory into Practice*, *41*(1), 26–32.

Scheuermann, J. (2018, January 25). *Group vs. collaborative learning: Knowing the difference makes a difference*. Faculty Focus Higher Ed.

Chapter 5

Legal Issues Impacting Social Media

OBJECTIVES

At the conclusion of this chapter you will be able to:

1. Understand legal issues impacting social media (ISTE 6).
2. Understand and describe some of the major employment laws associated with social media (ISTE 6).
3. Describe some of the implications of laws and legal issues impacting the conduct of employees, teachers, and students (ISTE 6).

LEGAL IMPLICATIONS OF SOCIAL MEDIA

The basis of social media legalities is rooted in the United States Constitution. The *Bill of Rights* comprised the first set of amendments that were adopted and ratified by the United States Congress in 1789 (United States Bill of Rights, 2018). The purpose of this document was to enumerate the freedoms given to all Americans, guarantee certain rights for citizens, and allow submission of grievances to the American government. Among this list of ten amendments, five of them have particular relevance to social media and are described in figure 5.1.

The first amendment is the one that probably has the biggest relevance to social media. This amendment states: "Congress shall make no law respecting an establishment of religion, or prohibiting the free exercise thereof; or abridging the freedom of speech, or of the press; or the right of the people peaceably to assemble, and to petition the Government for a redress of grievances" (United States Bill of Rights, 2018).

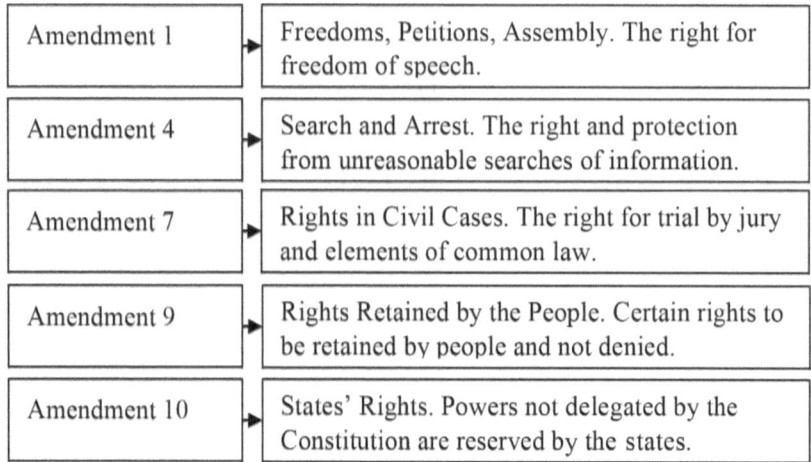

Figure 5.1. Major Bill of Rights Amendments impacting social media.

This amendment, in addition to allowing the right to practice religion, essentially provides the right to exercise *Freedom of Speech*. Americans have cherished this right of free expression. However, understanding exactly the full extent of this privilege, especially when it harms others, has been a subject of controversy. As a result, the extent and boundaries of free speech have been taken up by the United States' courts numerous times with varying rulings.

There have been myriad questions surrounding the right of free speech, what constitutes the limitations, and when free speech crosses the line into criminal offenses against others. For example, some of these associated criminal offenses include libel, defamation, slander, threats of violence, harassment, obscenity, and hate crimes. For some people, social media, under the guise of freedom of speech, can be a convenient weapon to cause harm to other people.

The use of social media has served to test the legalities of free speech. The courts continue to sort out when people have an inherent right to their speech and when their speech and conduct violates others' rights. For example, should school teachers or company employees be allowed to voice their negative opinions about their organization when they are employed by the organization? Likewise, should students or employees have the right to use social media to post defamatory statements about their teachers or employers?

And, what are the rights of parents and the community in posting comments about their school or local company? What should be the limitations of allowing people to express statements when they involve children and the public? Should people have the right to create public forums and use social media platforms to express political opinions that might negatively impact public officials or private employers?

For example, determining what exactly "speech" is can be tricky when used in social media. If a person clicks a "Like" button on a Facebook page that supports criminal activities, could this constitute a crime? Or, should this action be protected under the first amendment? Likewise, if a school teacher or company employee supports political activities on social media, does it constitute a violation of school district or company policy?

Another constitutional amendment that has significance to social media is the fourth amendment (see figure 5.1). This amendment states that: "The right of the people to be secure in their persons, houses, papers, and effects against unreasonable searches and seizures shall not be violated, and no warrants shall issue but upon probable cause, supported by oath or affirmation, and particularly describing the place to be searched and the persons or things to be seized" (United States Bill of Rights, 2018).

The fourth amendment protects people from unreasonable and warrantless searches by government, school districts, and other agencies into their personal information; however, how much confidentiality and reasonable considerations of non-investigatory actions can be unclear. The extent to which a person's information can be monitored and obtained under the interests of national security and then subsequently used against the person can be ambiguous. What are the powers and limits of the National Security Agency in monitoring and accessing a citizen's personal information?

For example, does the posting of provocative and explicit, sexual-based pictures by a school employee during off-work hours constitute a violation of school policy? And, does the school district have the right to monitor and seize this personal information? Likewise, do students or company employees have the right to prevent the intrusion by school or company authorities from using this personal information and taking punitive action against them? What are the boundaries that separate work-related actions and non-work actions? Do people have the right of confidentiality or is all personal information fair game for employers and officials when used on the World Wide Web?

Another controversial issue involves the extent upon which public employees can use social media to partake in political activities when their opinions are contrary to the interests of their employer or when their intention is to smear political figures. Laws have been established that provide guidelines on some aspects impacting the fourth amendment. For example, the United States Office of Special Counsel indicated that federal employees need to comply with the Hatch Act (Hatch Act, 2018).

This act essentially outlines that employees cannot engage in political activities during work hours including e-mails, chats, postings, and blogging. However, employees may be able, under certain restrictions, to partake in political activities using social media during nonwork hours. Also, this act provides less protection for employees who post damaging information on social media when it harms their employer.

Courts have tended to rule that information posted on public social media websites probably do not constitute a shield of private information and can be used against the person in legal cases. The essential argument is that people who post personal information for public viewing relinquish much of their protection and rights of confidentiality. Likewise, this public information is probably legally discoverable and admissible since the element of personal privacy is no longer a reasonable expectation.

However, the claim of privacy of information becomes less clear when information is posted on a social media site for viewing and is restricted for use only by invitation. For example, it may not be legal for a school teacher to obtain and repost pictures of a student when the pictures were obtained second-hand through friends of the student. Nor, is it probably legal or ethical to obtain this second-hand information through use of deceptive practices and fake names.

While the first and fourth amendments attach great significance to social media, the seventh, ninth, and tenth amendments have relevance as well (see figure 5.1.) The seventh amendment provides "common law" rights to people involved in civil suits and jury protections, the ninth amendment ensures that certain rights shall not be construed to deny or disparage others by the people, and the tenth amendment ensures that powers not granted by the United States government are reserved by the states. All these amendments afford users of social media basic inherent rights of protection and due process.

The extent to which a person whose rights have been violated can sue and claim monetary rewards for damages is also ambiguous. Do plaintiffs need to establish damage to obtain a monetary award? Or, if there is no harm, is there no foul? Plaintiffs may be able to seek a monetary claim solely based upon defamation or civil rights violations, but also may receive awards based upon emotional distress and resultant physical illness.

Along with these legal dilemmas comes the question, to what extent do lawyers have the right to social media postings during the litigation discovery stage? Generally the courts have tended to rule in favor of allowing social media postings to be relevant and accessible to reasonable "narrow" discovery during legal proceedings. The attempt to obtain information of a broad nature probably would not be reasonable and allowed.

However, in most cases, public postings likely can be subpoenaed from social media providers if the information is (or was) publically available. Information that is not public may require permission from the person posting the information. Moreover, it may not be legal, or ethical, for an attorney or litigant, to obtain private information from a social media website by deception, such as posing as a friend or using a fake name.

Another legal issue involves the unfair use of trademarks, propriety, and copyright-protected works. It is probably illegal and an ethical infringement to use this material without the owner's express written approval. This material (creative works) includes the use of songs, lyrics, photographs, book excerpts, digital forms, etc., for example, owners of songs often have the rights and control of their songs. The songs generally cannot be distributed, reprinted, reproduced, manipulated, or converted into other forms, displayed or digitally streamed without the owner's permission.

The doctrine of "fair use" may, in some circumstances, allow for the posting of limited creative works on social media websites. The United States copyright law allows for the use of copyrighted works if limited in scope and/or used for news reporting, education, and library archiving. For example, a teacher might be able to copy and post a limited amount of information (e.g., newspaper, article, or website) on a temporary, one-time, basis for the education of his or her students.

However, the teacher probably cannot copy a chapter from a copyrighted textbook intended to be sold to teachers or students and post it on a website to avoid buying the book. Some guiding principles that help to determine fair use include the intent and purpose of using the information, amount of information used, and effect of the use of creative works on the owner. Also, creative works published after 1923 may constitute fair use through the authority of *public domain*.

Another legal issue regarding copyright infringement liability includes the concept of *cease and desist*. Some social media site users and providers may be protected, to some degree, by the provision of "safe harbor" copyright laws. While it is best to seek permission to use copyrighted information, if site providers remove the information after receiving notice of cease and desist they may be protected from judgments. Social media users need to pay attention to the terms and conditions of copyright information and proper legal use. With the onset of *open source code* and free information easily available on the Internet, the temptations to violate copyright material may be increased.

Besides the many federal, state, and local laws and ordinances, practices of social media are also governed or influenced by myriad agencies and professional associations. Some of them include the Federal Trade Commission (FTC), Federal Communications Commission (FCC), National Security Agency (NSA), World Wide Web Consortium (W3C), and the Social Media Association (SMA).

For example, the FTC provides a variety of standards for corporate and educational institutions for the Internet and social media. Some of the areas involve use of intellectual property, social media campaigns and telemarketing, employment and labor laws, and posting of photographs and videos on the Internet. For example, blogging is a common practice used in social media. However, bloggers who receive compensation for endorsing products and services generally must disclose that they are being compensated for these actions.

Educators and company managers have authority and influence over their students and employees. They need to recognize the boundaries in recommending products and services when they are receiving compensation for their so-called advertisement postings. The FTC frowns upon social media users who engage in "flogging"—practices that appear to be objective postings, but typically are self-serving and misleading. Severe financial penalties, and per infractions, can be assessed to organizations that don't follow federal guidelines.

EMPLOYMENT LAWS AND IMPLICATIONS

There are many federal and state laws that impact the use of social media and employment. These laws generally apply to the employment practices of all students and employees when using the Internet and social media. For example, the use of social media websites is becoming increasingly more popular in the recruiting, screening, selection, and employment of people.

Open positions, whether part-time jobs for students or full-time company positions, are routinely posted on social media websites and are governed by the same standards, policies, and laws as traditional face-to-face processes. All employers and job seekers need to be aware of these laws, as well as state and local laws and statutes that apply to all employment practices.

The basis of many of the current federal laws has its roots from the civil rights movement of the 1960s. One of the landmark agencies of this time was the *Equal Employment Opportunity Commission* (EEOC) which was established by *Title VII of the 1964 Civil Rights Act*. The original act prohibited discrimination on the basis of race, color, relation, national origin, and gender.

This civil rights law covered all aspects of employment including planning, hiring, supervising, compensation, job classification, promotions, training, retirement, and termination. While the *Civil Rights Act* primarily pertains to employers and public and private institutions with fifteen or more employees, it is a good practice for all organizations to follow these laws.

The act provides the basis for bringing litigation against institutions that practice discriminatory acts. This federal law was created to serve all "protected classes" of employees which mainly consisted of women, African Americans, Asians, Hispanics, Indians, and Eskimos. While there are many federal employment antidiscrimination laws, there are also many other state and local laws that also need to be followed when using social media for employment practices. People need to contact their state and local agencies to learn about these laws.

In addition to the original laws of the Civil Rights Act, subsequent amendments have been made to the act such as protecting individuals above forty, disabled people, and pregnant women. Also, in 1978, the EEOC adopted other guidelines to protect claims of reverse discrimination practices as an outgrowth of affirmative action. Essentially, the act stated that organizations should avoid selection policies that have an adverse impact on hiring or employment opportunities because of race, gender, or ethnicity unless there is an organizational necessity for the practice.

The penalties associated with *Civil Rights Act* violations can be severe. The law allows individuals who have been discriminated against to seek compensatory and punitive damages for both willful and intentional discrimination acts. Compensatory damages generally involve harm to an employee for pain and emotional suffering. Punitive damages can be assessed against an employer which serves as punishment and a deterrent for others.

There are some limitations for judgment awards depending upon the size of an organization. In addition to the EEOC, violations of discrimination are also enforced and judgments can be awarded by state human rights commissions. For example, the State of Illinois has a Department of Human Rights Commission which is responsible for protecting individuals from discriminatory practices (Illinois Department of Human Rights, 2018).

Both the EEOC and state human rights commissions have the authority to assess monetary penalties and both of these agencies have established time frames in which a claim can be filed. For example, the State of Illinois typically allows for 180 days from the occurrence and the EEOC allows 300 days. Not only can an organization incur financial awards for acts of discrimination but they can also incur significant emotional pain, defense costs, work disruption, wasted time, and resources defending claims. Therefore, organizations are wise to follow legal practices and avoid claims of discrimination.

Let's review some of the key federal laws and how they can impact social media (see table 5.1). The first law is the Civil Rights Act of 1964 which prohibits discrimination on factors such as race, color, relation, national origin, gender, disability, and retaliation. The posting of jobs for students and perspective employees must follow legal guidelines and avoid phrases such as "men wanted for school construction work" or "energetic women desired for part-time school assemblies," which may be violations of the law.

In fact, when posting a job on a social media website it may be advisable to include an antidiscrimination phrase such as "We are an equal opportunity employer and we do not discriminate against people and we take affirmative action measures to ensure against employment discrimination in all phases of

Table 5.1. Major Federal and EEOC Laws and Executive Orders Impacting Social Media

Law	Basic Description
Title VII of the Civil Rights Act of 1964 as amended	Prohibits discrimination on the basis of race, color, religion, national origin, gender, pregnancy, childbirth, and retaliation.
Equal Pay Act of 1963	Prohibits pay discrimination against males and females who perform equal work that is substantially the same.
Title IV of the Education Amendments of 1972	Prohibits discrimination against males and females in activities and programs receiving federal funding and grants.
Rehabilitation Act of 1973 Sections 501 and 505	Prohibits discrimination against qualified disabled people who can perform the major functions of a job and affirmative action to employ and promote qualified disabled people.
Title VII, Section 1604, Sexual Harassment Act	Prohibits unwelcome sexual advances, requests for sexual favors, and other verbal or physical conduct of a sexual nature that creates a hostile or offensive work environment.
Age Discrimination in Employment Act 1967 (ADEA)	Protects people who are forty or older from age discrimination or retaliation for filing a complaint.
Title I Americans with Disabilities Act of 1990 (ADA)	Protects disabled people from employment discrimination or retaliation for filing a complaint.

Source: U.S. EEOC, www.gov/laws, 2018.

employment including, but not limited to, recruiting, advertising, selecting, employing, compensating, promoting, terminating and other conditions of employment against job applicants and employees on the basis of race, creed, color, national origin, gender, and other discriminatory factors."

Another example of an antidiscrimination law is the *Equal Pay Act of 1963* (see table 5.1). This law was an outgrowth to the Fair Labor Standards Act. This law prohibits compensation discrimination of people who have the same skills and experiences and are performing the same job. However, there can be several exceptions to pay differences such as bonuses for higher performances, seniority, merit, working conditions, geographic differences, and quality and quantity of work.

The law primarily serves to protect differences in pay between men and women who are substantially doing the same work, and have the same qualifications, performance, and seniority. For example, this law could be potentially violated when using social media to post jobs on LinkedIn. LinkedIn has been a popular social media site to seek job opportunities, as well as explore career advancement. LinkedIn, in fact, openly states that it is committed to equal employment opportunity and publishes this statement on its website.

With this in mind, employers need to be careful and avoid discriminatory practices such as posting job openings that exclude people, especially those of a protected group. However, controversies can evolve regarding the inclusion of personal photos and graduation dates when posting resumes. The use of photos could potentially allow employers to screen candidates based upon racial characteristics. Likewise, the inclusion of employment and graduation dates could also allow employers to potentially screen younger candidates for positions.

Title IV of the Education Amendments Act of 1972 prohibits discrimination on the basis of gender for educational programs by recipients of federal financial assistance. The act states that "No persons in the United States shall, on the basis of sex, be excluded from participating in, be denied the benefits of, or be subjected to discrimination under any program or activity receiving federal financial assistance" (United States Equal Employment Opportunity Commission, 2018).

This law requires organizations and school districts to maintain internal procedures for federal grants and resolving complaints of discrimination. In addition, Title IV also applies to programs of a school district regardless of whether the program is federally funded. With the advent of charter and private schools, enforcing Title IV has been somewhat controversial, but recognizing and adhering to this law may be in the best interests of all organizations to prevent law suits and questions of equality, fairness, and fiscal management.

For example, the violation of this Title IV could occur when an employer intentionally or unintentionally posts learning opportunities, jobs, events, or clubs that might discriminate against members of a protected group. Something as innocent as posting of an after-school event only for white students on Facebook may be entirely inappropriate by excluding students of other races. Likewise, a company needs to be sensitive about singling out only one race to post advertisements, which may alienate or offend others.

The Rehabilitation Act of 1973 serves to promote equality for employees with disabilities. This law requires that employers take affirmative action to recruit, hire, and promote qualified disabled people. The law serves to protect disabled persons who can perform the main functions of the job with reasonable accommodations. While the law has good intentions, some employers may have difficulty interpreting exactly what "reasonable accommodations" means.

The law does not mandate that accommodations be made if it imposes a significant hardship or monetary expense that is unreasonable for a company or school district. If an organization is located in an old and poorly designed building, it may be difficult and unreasonable to expect management to install an elevator if, by doing so, it creates a significant hardship and, in some cases, could bankrupt the organization.

However, in many cases management can accommodate disabled employees through actions such as modifying work schedules, providing ergonomic devices, and other special equipment or modifications, to support a disabled person in performing the primary functions of a job. The use of social media technology can also impact this law. Using the computer by disabled students, especially, for education and learning, may need reasonable accommodations such as visual, physical, and ergonomic support for work stations.

The EEOC included a sexual harassment amendment in 1980 to the Title VII Civil Rights Act. This law prohibits *sexual harassment* in the workplace (see table 5.1). The law states that sexual harassment involves "Unwelcome sexual advances, requests for sexual favors, and other verbal or physical conduct of a sexual nature—when such conduct has the purpose or effect of unreasonably interfering with an individual's work performance or creating an intimidating, hostile or offensive working environment" (United States Equal Employment Opportunity Commission, 2018).

There are several types of sexual harassment discrimination in this amendment. *Adverse impact discrimination* involves the unintentional actions that have negative or detrimental effects against a person or group of people. For example, this discrimination might involve requiring certain height requirements that could unintentionally discriminate against people of a certain ethnicity.

Adverse treatment discrimination involves the intentional act of treating people differently. An example of this discrimination could be the unrelenting posting of messages from a person on social media such as Facebook to another person that becomes harassing based upon sex or using social media to post sexually explicit photos of people on the site.

Retaliation is an intentional discrimination when an employer commits an adverse action against the employee because he or she has complained against discrimination or filed a discrimination claim. An example of a more ambiguous situation may involve employees who post negative comments on social media websites against their organization and incur retaliation. The question becomes: Was the organizational action against the employee a violation of organizational policy or simply retaliation?

An example of quid pro quo could be when a manager requests sexual favors from an employee in exchange for a good performance rating or promotion. This would be discriminatory whether done either in person or using social media. Another type of sexual harassment discrimination is called *environmental sexual harassment* referred to as *hostile working environment*.

This type of harassment involves any unreasonable actions that interfere with an employee's work performance that have a sexual basis. Examples might include verbal, physical, and visual sexual actions, patently offensive conduct, harassment of individuals because of their gender, displaying inappropriate sexual pictures on social media, or sending sexually based content e-mails.

Sexual harassment complaints have significantly increased over the past years. Organizations are required to post sexual harassment policies, conduct investigations when complaints have been received, take action against offenders, conduct training for employees, and provide an employee complaint mechanism or grievance system. Many state laws have similar provisions to the Federal Title VII amendment. Sexual harassment discrimination has become a complex law and all employers should consult legal counsel.

The Age Discrimination in Employment Act (ADEA) of 1967 was designed to prohibit age discrimination for employees over forty years of age in planning, recruiting, selection, training, promoting, transferring, compensating, and other practices of employment (see table 5.1). The intention of the law is to prevent companies from discharging or refusing to hire older workers based upon their age. In 1986, this act was amended to prohibit discrimination in retirement for people above forty years of age.

An example of this law would include a manager using social media to encourage a competent sixty-year-old employee to retire or making age-related comments to the person. It should be noted that this law protects people who are forty years of age or older but does not protect people who are under the age of forty. It is never a good practice to hire or fire people based upon age rather than performance factors and needs of the organization. Also, because of this law many organizations have offered early retirement programs in an effort to encourage retirement, reduce costs, and to avoid potential discrimination practices.

The Americans with Disabilities Act of 1990 (ADA) Title I was established to prevent discrimination against disabled individuals who can perform the essential functions of a job with reasonable accommodations. This law generally applies to employers who have fifty or more employees. This law has had significant impact on school districts and companies given that it covers such a wide range of medical conditions such as HIV, mental illnesses, learning disabilities, alcohol and drug addiction, and other physical ailments.

This law is executed under the EEOC and was subsequently amended to prohibit school districts from discrimination regardless of the number of employees. Concerning this law, it is critical for any organization to not only prevent adverse actions by the EEOC, but also to avoid civil law suits by individuals. Adherence to these laws and policies and taking proactive measures can avoid the heartache of a potential costly defense.

For example, if an educator is using social media in the classroom, or online learning platform, special accommodations might be needed for students with disabilities who may have difficulty in using the computer and equipment. It is required that the school district provide special support and resources for students with special needs. Moreover, a case could be made that it is the right thing to do from a moral and ethical standpoint.

In addition to the Civil Rights Act, employees, including students, have legal responsibilities to comply with federal, state, and school district policies in using social media related to employment practices. For example, the National Labor Relations Act (NLRA) was established in 1935 to encourage the private sector workers and employers to work together in a productive environment. The intent of the act was to curtail work stoppages, general conflict, and strikes that can be harmful to the economy and welfare of the United States.

With this in mind, the NLRA has established numerous guidelines for workers and employers, as well as laws and policies that help govern employment practices. For example, the NLRA has outlined a variety of social media guidelines for employees to follow (see textbox 5.1).

The intention of these guidelines is to help workers and employers understand what actions might constitute violations and infringements of employees' rights under the NLRA.

TEXTBOX 5.1. EXAMPLES OF SOCIAL MEDIA GUIDELINES BY THE NATIONAL LABOR RELATIONS ACT

- Federal law protects your right to engage in not only union activity, but also "protected concerted" activity. Using social media is a form of "protected activity."
- You have the right to address work-related issues and share information about pay, benefits, and working conditions with coworkers and with a union. You have the right to take action with one of more coworkers to improve your working conditions.
- You have the right to address work-related issues with coworkers using Facebook, YouTube, and other social media.
- Individually griping about some aspect of work is not "concerted activity" and what you say must have some relation to group action or seek to initiate, induce, or prepare for group action or bring a group complaint to the attention of management.

> - You don't have the right to say things about your employer that are egregiously offensive or knowingly and deliberately false, or if you publicly disparage your employer's products or services without relating your complaints to any labor controversy.

For example, the intent of the NLRA guidelines is to allow workers to engage in "protected concerted" activities such as addressing work-related issues and the sharing of information about their pay, benefits, work conditions, and other work items. However, the use of social media to post gripes and egregious insults against an organization, especially knowing the posts are false, is prohibited. Moreover, employees are generally not protected in making publically disparaging comments about an organization's products or services.

Based upon myriad federal and state laws and policies, school districts and companies need to be aware of practices that might violate the rights of students and employees. For example, inquiries about clubs, organizations, and societies of a job applicant may be unlawful unless proven that it is relevant to the job. Any questions, which may violate the applicant's race, sex, national origin, disability status, age, religion, color, or ancestry generally should be avoided.

A summary of limitations on preemployment inquiries include:

- Health and medical examinations
- Credit ratings and economic status
- Race and ethnicity
- Religious affiliation
- Disabilities
- Marital status and family
- Gender
- Arrest records
- Security background checks not relevant to the job
- Citizenship
- Military status and obligations

Keep in mind that an employer is generally not liable for employees' nonwork postings on a social media website when conducted on their own personal time and equipment. An employer, or school district, may not, in most cases, be entitled to monitor or view employees' or students' personal social media postings. But an organization may have an obligation for taking action when the postings involve the organization and a complaint or legal case has been filed. EEOC allegations or violations of discrimination, libel, harassment, and defamation are examples All complaints of this nature are required to entail an investigation and appropriate actions need to be taken when violations occur (National Labor Relations Act, 2018).

STUDENT LEGAL ISSUES

The negative impact of using social media to harm students should be a concern to the entire community, as well as the school district. Wide attention has been given to the use of social media by students and the potential for abuse. While there are some obvious situations of abuse, there are also no clear-cut boundaries. In some respects, the courts are still not in total agreement regarding student discipline and conduct in public schools.

The essential guideline for students and their rights of freedom of speech is that students cannot engage in activities that disrupt the work, learning, and discipline of the school. The interpretation of this statement and perceptions can be ambiguous when determining when a student has violated this guideline. One difficulty is determining the boundaries where school activities begin and end; for example, when students use social media outside the school environment, but the content is related to school, it can be ambiguous.

The dilemma occurs when students use social media after school hours and outside the school environment but the posting of content has a direct negative effect on other students, educators, staff, or the school. The question that can be posed: Do school authorities have the right to monitor or intrude into a student's personal social media space? One argument is that a student's social media posts are protected by the first amendment. However, if it can be shown that the student's actions are somehow disrupting, threatening, or defaming others at the school the student probably won't be protected by the first amendment.

A case can be made that if students post photos or information on social media that directly relate to school functions and educational activities then they probably have less protection by the first amendment. For example, if a student takes pictures or videos of educators or fellow students and displays them on social media that portrays them in a derogatory manner the student's action probably does not constitute free speech (*Requa v. Kent School District*, United States Courts Archive, 2018).

Another situation involves the posting of personal photos of oneself showing unprofessional behavior such as excessive drinking or use of illegal substances. In these cases the person probably runs the risk of these photos being used to reject the person from employment or admittance into professional societies or universities. The person probably can't claim protection from the first amendment (United States Department of Education Social Media Laws and Guidance, 2018).

Guidelines on the posting of content on social media websites have been offered by educational associations and federal agencies. For example, the United States Department of Education provides that following guidelines for the removal of content that undermines the respect or dignity of their employees or agency. These include content that:

- Contain vulgar or abusive language, personal attacks or any kind, or offensive terms that target specific ethnic or racial groups;
- Promote services or products (noncommercial links that are relevant to the blog post or comment are acceptable);
- Are clearly "off topic" or are "spam";
- Make unsupported accusations;
- Reference federal employees by name;
- Violate the laws of the United States or the policies of the United States Department of Education.

The action of *bullying* and *stalking* using social media should not be tolerated in schools. Most schools have anti-bullying and stalking policies and other codes of conduct. The hurt and emotional harm that can be done by these actions can have long-lasting impact on victims. Some examples of these actions include posting unauthorized pictures and videos of students, abusive comments, hacking or fraudulently executing posts through other names and venues, and making intimidating and threatening statements.

People can become victims of harassment by face-to-face contact or through the Internet. Federal and state laws provide protection to people from harassment which generally includes obscene comments with the intent of offending, threatening, or creating a hostile environment to others. In addition to harassment, extortion, and stealing of nonconsensual material by a perpetrator's interception may constitute criminal and civil liability. These actions may also violate federal interstate commerce laws. Severe penalties can be given to these offenders.

Another common criminal act is the case of *defamation* of school educators, staff, and other students. Using hate blogs on websites or Twitter to defame others can result in severe penalties and civil action. Defamation is not reserved to only newspapers, radio, or television, but can be done through any type of communication media, and it doesn't matter how many people are exposed to the defamation.

A serious issue that impacts social media is the posting of *threats* against other people and an organization. The courts have wrestled with what social media postings constitute a viable threat. Students who make open threats that reasonably can be construed as legitimate run the risk of being prosecuted. Moreover, *threats of violence* and shootings must be taken seriously and investigated.

Some guidelines in handling school threats include:

- Investigate and pursue all threats immediately.
- Contact appropriate police and law enforcement for support.
- Administer disciplinary and criminal action against the offenders.
- Document all actions taken and keep detailed records.
- Provide ongoing training for educators in dealing with threats.
- Ensure safety and security measures for all students and people.

The best policy to take in using social media is to treat each other with respect and dignity. All social media users should review and understand organizational policies, local community ordinances, and state and federal laws governing social media actions and conduct. The temptation to violate these policies and laws may come with severe penalties and damage not only to others but the perpetrators themselves.

SUMMARY

The primary goal of federal and state laws is to provide protection and guidelines for people and organizations to understand what are acceptable legal practices and this relates to social media as well. The basis of social media legal issues is rooted in the United States Constitution. The *Bill of Rights* comprised the first set of amendments that were adopted and ratified by the United States Congress in 1789.

The first, fourth, seventh, ninth, and tenth amendments are amendments that have particular relevance to social media. The first amendment ensures freedom of speech, the fourth provides limited privacy, and the seventh amendment provides "common law" rights to people involved in civil suits and jury protections. The ninth amendment ensures that certain rights shall not be construed to deny or disparage others by the people, and the tenth amendment ensures that powers not granted by the United States government are reserved by the states.

There are also several guidelines by the NLRA board such as providing an allowance for workers to engage in "protected concerted" activities. Some of these include addressing work-related issues and the sharing of information about their pay and benefits and work conditions. However, employees are not protected in using social media to post gripes and egregious insults against their organization, especially knowing the posts are false.

There are a number of federal and state laws that relate to conduct of students and employees in using social media. Some of these include avoiding harassment, stalking, bullying, defamation, libel, and threats. All organizations, employees, and students need to stay current with federal and state laws, and organizational policies. Good communication is a key to social media legal issues.

CASE STUDY

Institutional Social Media Policy—Creating a Workable Plan

Your organization is experiencing myriad social media issues involving all employees and constituents. Some of the issues include violations of federal and state laws and policies, lack of adherence to social media association guidelines, and conflicts among management regarding understanding of the organization's policies on social media use.

Therefore, the board of your organization has requested that you investigate and analyze your current organizational practices and then develop a social media policy for all people to follow. Therefore, you are to create an outline (with examples) of what this social media policy should include.

In creating this social media policy, include such items as:

1. Types of federal and state laws and executive orders.
2. Types of guidelines from various social media associations.
3. How key United States *Bill of Rights* amendments impact social media.
4. Involvement of FTC, FTA, and other agencies.
5. Examples of dos and don'ts in using social media.
6. What to do when you suspect a violation of social media policies.
7. Management of oversight of social media policies and enforcement.

EXERCISES AND DISCUSSION QUESTIONS

1. List and describe examples of the key United States *Bill of Rights* amendments and how they can be controversial in applying them to social media.
2. Describe some to the National Labor Relations Act guidelines for employees in using social media.
3. Suggest some precautions and guidelines for all learning and professional development in your organization when using social media.
4. Interview a social media administrator, and identify some of the typical issues he or she experiences and ideas for improving the use of social media in an organization.

REFERENCES

Hatch Act. (2018). Retrieved July 9, 2018, from htttps://osc.gov/Pages/HatchAct.aspx

Illinois Department of Human Rights. (2018). State of Illinois, US/DHR.

National Labor Relations Act. (2018). Retrieved July 9, 2018, from www.NLRA.gov

Requa v. Kent School District, United States Courts Archive. (2018). Retrieved July 9, 2018, from https://www.loc.gov/rr/program/bib/ourdocs/billofrights.html

United States Bill of Rights. (2018). Retrieved July 9, 2018, from https://www.unitedstatescourts.org/federal/wawd/143664/

United States Department of Education Social Media Laws and Guidance. (2018). Retrieved July 9, 2018, from https://www2.ed.gov/about/overview/focus/facebook-comments.html

United States Equal Employment Opportunity Commission. (2018). Retrieved July 9, 2018, from www.eeoc.gov/laws

Chapter 6

Evaluation and Moving Forward

OBJECTIVES

1. Identify methods for evaluating learning experiences that use social media or collaboration tools (ISTE 2).
2. Analyze evaluation results to make decisions about implementing social media and collaboration tools for learning (ISTE 2, 5).
3. Create a plan to evaluate learning experiences that use social media and collaboration tools using a survey, cognitive walkthrough, and pilot study (ISTE 2, 5).

SURVEYING STAKEHOLDERS

Few would argue that technology changes and grows exponentially. In fact, Gordon Moore, cofounder of the Intel Corporation, said in 1965 that the number of transistors in a dense integrated circuit would double every two years (Intel Corporation, n.d.). This is now known as Moore's Law. Many believe this principle applies to the exponential rate of growth seen with other technologies, including social media and collaboration tools.

Educators, trainers, curriculum designers, and instructional designers have begun to harness social media and collaboration tools in new and exciting ways. Even though some of these tools were not initially intended for professional or academic use, they are often integrated into classrooms, workplaces, and play spaces for the purposes of enhancing or creating learning experiences.

It is a good practice to test the waters with new technologies and tools for learning. What at first may seem like a wonderful new technology may turn out to be a dud. What may seem like a dud at first may eventually be modified and improved to suit the needs of the users. This is why evaluation is a necessity.

The first step in evaluation is to establish evaluation goals. This can begin by answering the question: What needs to be evaluated and why? For example, if a teacher is considering integrating a social media tool in her classroom, she may have a goal to "learn more about her colleagues' experiences of social media tools in their classrooms." She may also want to conduct an evaluation of a specific tool to "determine if the social media tool is appropriate for her classroom's needs." Lastly, she may wish to compare two tools in a real-life learning activity in her own classroom to "identify which social media tool is most effective in reaching learning outcomes."

There are several methods for reaching these goals and conducting effective assessments and evaluations of technologies, tools, processes, systems, and practices in the learning and development, education technology, and instructional design fields. Three methods covered in this chapter include:

1. Surveying stakeholders,
2. Completing a cognitive walkthrough,
3. Conducting a pilot study with a small group.

This is not an exhaustive list, but a good place to start. Small organizations often do not have the resources to do a comprehensive needs assessment or evaluation. These three methods can provide important information about the needs, usage, effectiveness, and efficiency of a technology or tool such as social media or collaboration in a learning, teaching, or training situation.

Anytime a new process, practice, concept, or tool may be put into place, it is important to talk to people to determine beliefs, behaviors, values, and many other factors. These conversations can happen formally or informally, in person or virtually, and using a variety of methods. Some methods for talking to people include surveys, interviews, and focus groups.

It is also important to decide on the people who are the key stakeholders for any project before initiating conversations. These are the people who will make decisions, develop budgets, create activities, implement plans and activities, or otherwise take part in the project. Audiences for projects related to teaching and learning with technology might include:

- Learners (students, employees, trainees)
- Facilitators
- Teachers
- Trainers
- Instructional designers

- Curriculum designers
- Learning and development staff
- Human resources staff
- Managers
- Supervisors
- Superintendents
- Principals
- Chief learning officers (CLOs)
- Chief information officers (CIOs)
- Technology specialists
- Budget control officers
- Systems administrators
- Technology coaches
- Communities of practice (professional associations, LinkedIn groups)
- Professional organizations
- Politicians and policy administrators
- Community members
- Popular audiences (Facebook, personal networks)

Once the key stakeholders are identified, a series of questions and key discussion points can be developed that will help to meet the goals established for the evaluation. Below is an example of a survey study, including the study goal, participant group, survey questions, and survey results with general discussion of each result.

To gauge the general beliefs and opinions of a professional audience around social media and collaboration tools for learning and teaching, an exploratory study was conducted from February 15 to March 15, 2018. An eight-question survey was distributed on LinkedIn to nine professional groups associated with training and education.

More specifically, the goal of this survey was to get a sense of these individuals' perceptions about social media and collaboration tools for learning, teaching, or training. Ninety-two individuals responded to the survey. Responses to these questions as well as some comparisons among these data to demonstrate potential relationships between variables are presented.

1. In which of these fields do you work or have you worked most recently?

Forty-three percent of participants said they work in higher education, 24 percent work in K–12 education, 24 percent work in corporate, and 9 percent work in nonprofit. No participants identified as working for government or other (see figure 6.1).

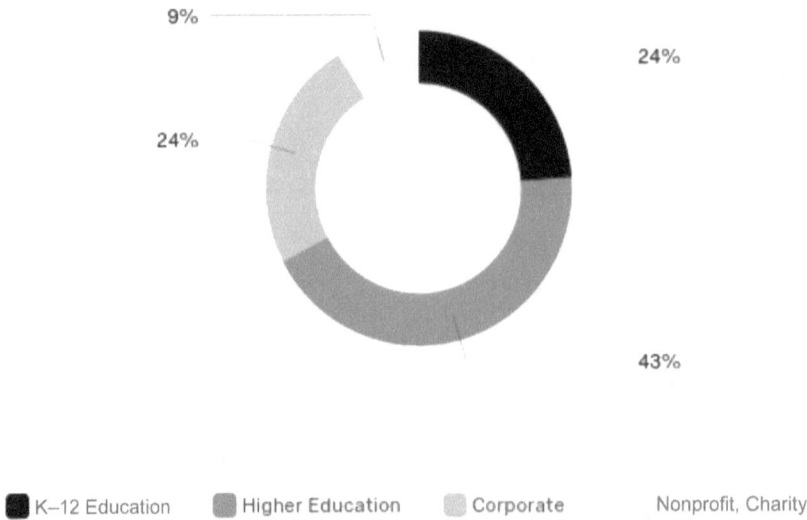

Figure 6.1. Summary of responses to Question 1: respondents' field/professional area.

It is possible that there were nearly twice as many participants in higher education as compared to K–12 education because higher education employees were more frequently using LinkedIn during the month of the study. It is also possible that the nine LinkedIn groups that were sent the survey contained more higher education employees than the other groups.

2. Social media tools such as LinkedIn, Twitter, and Facebook can support learning, training, and/or teaching if used appropriately (Scale: Strongly Agree to Strongly Disagree).

Eighty percent of participants agreed or strongly agreed with this statement, though only 30 percent strongly agreed. Fifteen percent were neutral, 7 percent disagreed, and 0 percent strongly disagreed with this statement (see figure 6.2).

In general, the participants seem to agree that social media does have a place in learning or training situations. However, compared to a similar question about collaboration tools for learning, training, or teaching asked below, participants seemed less confident about social media tools.

3. I have used social media tools for the purposes of learning, teaching, or training in the past year (True or False).

Sixty-nine percent of participants have used social media for learning, teaching, or training recently (see figure 6.3), and 31 percent have not.

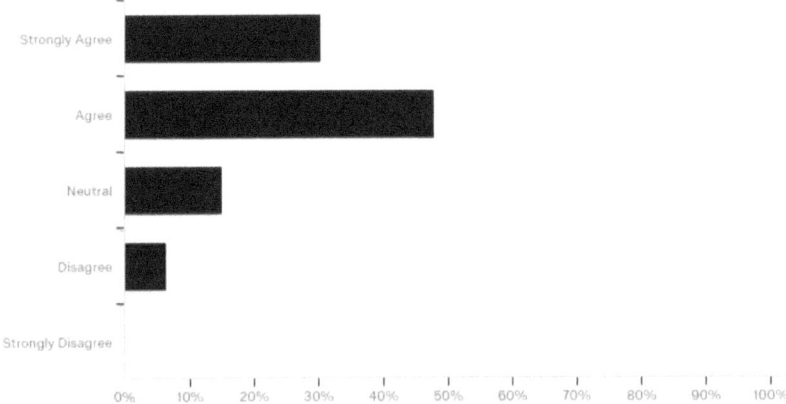

Figure 6.2. Summary of responses to Question 2: Social media tools can support learning, teaching, or training.

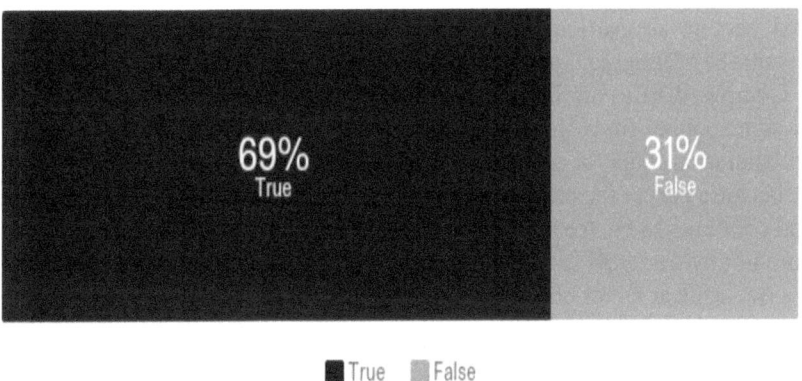

Figure 6.3. Summary of responses to Question 3: I have used social media tools for learning, teaching, or training, in the past year.

While these data suggest that social media tools do have a place in learning, teaching, or training currently, the ratio is still quite different compared to a similar question asked of participants regarding collaboration tools instead of social media tools. This could be due to the population of people who do not use social media frequently; who have given it up; or who use it only for personal, entertainment, or leisure purposes.

Another hypothesis is that the responses to this question and the previous question are related. Perhaps those participants who responded in the negative do not believe social media can support learning, teaching, or training "because" they have not used it for that purpose previously. However, that causal relationship cannot be determined without further questioning of the participants.

4. I have learned something new while using social media tools in the past year (True or False).

Ninety percent of participants answered "True," and 10 percent answered "False" (see figure 6.4). This question was asked of participants to see if they themselves experienced learning through use of social media. It is encouraging to see that most people do and shows promise for continuing to leverage the features of social media for learning, teaching, and training.

5. Collaboration tools such as Google Drive, GoToMeeting, and Skype can support learning, training, and/or teaching if used appropriately (Scale: Strongly Agree to Strongly Disagree).

Seventy-eight percent of participants selected "Strongly Agree." Twenty-two percent of participants selected "Agree." Zero participants selected "Neutral," "Disagree," or "Strongly disagree" (see figure 6.5).

Compared to a similar question about social media tools asked earlier, these responses show that participants feel more strongly about the value of collaboration tools for supporting learning, training, or teaching. This could be because part of the original intent of many of these collaboration tools was, and continues to be, for learning or training purposes. Social media tools were not initially designed for these purposes, so their usefulness and effectiveness are not as clear as for collaboration tools.

6. I have used collaboration tools for the purposes of learning, teaching, or training in the past year (True or False).

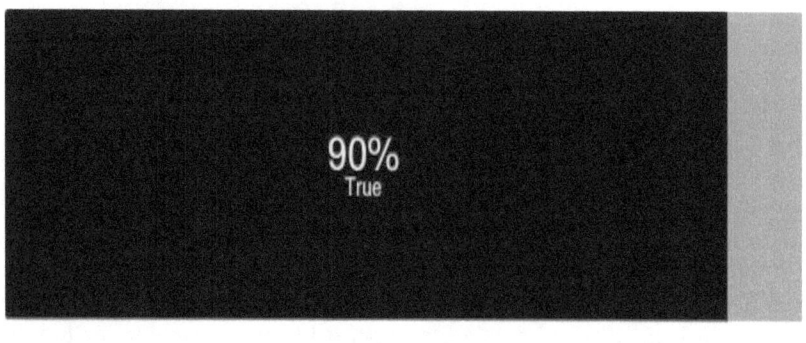

Figure 6.4. Summary of responses to Question 4: I learned something new using social media tools in the past year.

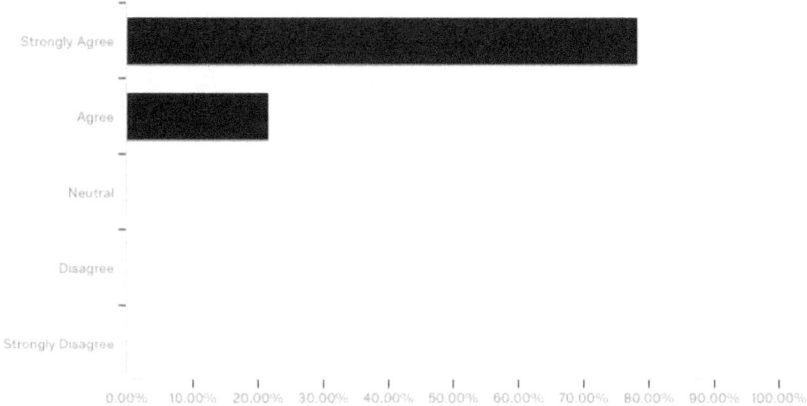

Figure 6.5. Summary of responses to Question 5: Collaboration tools can support learning, teaching, or training.

Almost all of participants (98 percent) said this statement was true for them. A hypothesis could be that participants' recent experiences with collaboration tools noted in this question is related to their beliefs about the value of the tools for supporting learning, teaching, or training mentioned in the previous question (see figure 6.6). In other words, they may have had a good learning experience that helped them recognize the value of collaboration tools for learning and training. Again, this is not conclusive and a causal relationship cannot be determined from these survey questions alone.

7. I have learned something new while using collaboration tools in the past year (True or False).

This statement was true for 96 percent of participants. These results could suggest that collaboration tools are effectively used for learning, teaching, or training situations (see figure 6.7).

8. Comment about your experience with social media or collaboration tools for learning/teaching/training (Optional).

Participants left a variety of comments in this field of the survey. Some of the responses were as follows:

"If done right, with the right goals and focus I believe they can be incredibly useful as long as they are not used just for the sake of using them."—Participant 2

"Collaboration tools help me interact with people that I am learning from. Social media seems to only have people trash talking, exaggerating how great their life is, half-truths, and junk: advertisements and games."—Participant 7

Figure 6.6. Summary of responses to Question 6: I used collaboration tools for learning, teaching, or training in the past year.

Figure 6.7. Responses to Question 7: I learned something new using collaboration tools in the past year.

"When collaboration needs to happen outside the classroom, these are some of the resources available to support learning."—Participant 24

"These tools focus on user-generated content allowing the learner to use his/her device to contribute to his/her learning. I have used social media for crowd sourcing (ask a bunch of ppl about one topic and see the variety of response examples), record an experience or how to do something, share it and see the variety of comments (learner feedback)."—Participant 31

"I love social media for collaboration. Twitter has helped me so much with professional development and getting ideas for my classroom!"—Participant 47

"Very few aspects in which social media can support learning significantly! I normally use Wechat to answer to some queries from my students"—Participant 48

"Social Media can be a tool for collaborative learning. It provides a scope of information, perspectives, insight and influence. It shouldn't be a sole source for learning but certainly has its place, especially in adult learning/corporate learning."—Participant 59

"I have only used social media for learning/training minimally, but have used collaboration tools frequently."—Participant 60

"I haven't used social media tools for teaching/learning/training but have heard that it can be a great resource for a community of practitioners. I use

Google Drive, ZOOM Meeting, and GoToMeeting for collaborating with colleagues all over the country."—Participant 63

"As a student, I use Zoom and Google Docs a lot!"—Participant 78

"My concern with Social Media tools for academics is security."—Participant 80

"No direct experience yet, but I am interested in research that speaks to the use of social media technology within a games-based learning environment. For instance, when I level is completed, or learning outcome is achieved, that can be shared to the student's social media account as an achievement badge."—Participant 82

"We use Slack extensively."—Participant 86

"I'm fairly certain that most of my learning about educational technology comes from social media—either a Facebook group that I'm in posting new things or a tweet that I follow to an article, I'm not sure how teachers kept up to date without social media."—Participant 89

"LinkedIn is a useful learning tool—I teach writing, so LI is basically similar to an online resume and can help students learn how to promote themselves through writing. It's also a critical job search tool, so it's practical beyond a classroom education! I cannot speak much to other forms of social media, although I do use Skype to tutor students."—Participant 93

Reviewing the qualitative responses to this question helps to back up some of the quantitative data. It also gives some insight into what the participants need, like, dislike, or have experienced that is important to them. However, it cannot prove any causal relationships without more information.

It also cannot provide conclusive evidence of any phenomena across a population because the sample size would need to be larger. Nevertheless, the survey helps to meet the larger goal of determining general thoughts and beliefs about social media and collaboration tools. It can help drive next steps for research into this area.

COMPLETING A COGNITIVE WALKTHROUGH

Another common method of evaluation used in the educational technology and instructional design fields is a cognitive walkthrough. This is a method that is borrowed from the user experience (UX) field where software and hardware are tested on a regular basis. The key components of a cognitive walkthrough are shown in figure 6.8.

A cognitive walkthrough involves an evaluator (or designer, facilitator, or teacher) asking a small sample of users (or learners, in this case) to work through an activity or task step by step (Spencer, 2000). The evaluator observes what happens during this walkthrough to catch any errors, "bugs, or obstacles in the activity, system, or tool."

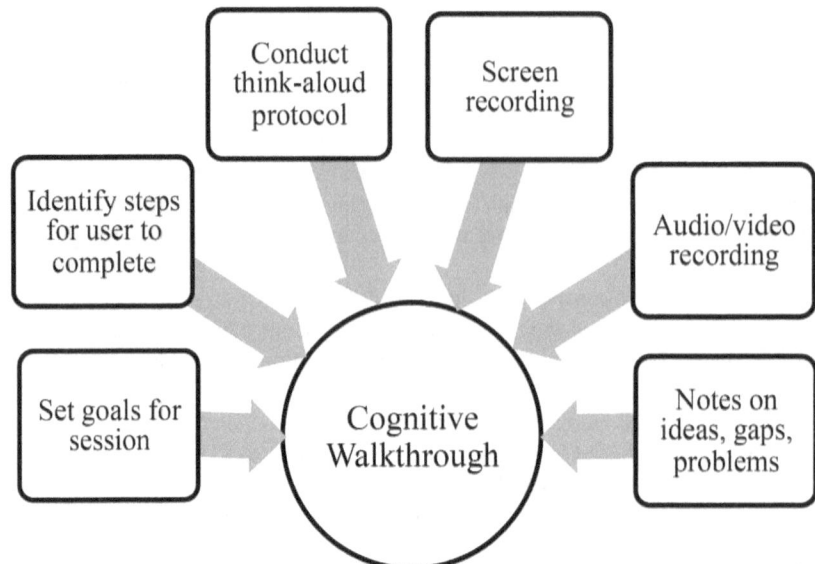

Figure 6.8. Components of a cognitive walkthrough.

The most recent version of a cognitive walkthrough asks the evaluator to answer two questions for each step of a task: "1. Will the user know what to do at this step?" and "2. If the user does the right thing, will they know that they did the right thing, and are making progress towards their goal?" (Spencer, 2000, p. 355).

Often the evaluator has the user follow a think-aloud protocol during a cognitive walkthrough. A think-aloud protocol is simply having the users explain what they are doing as they are doing it. If using an app or other type of software, the evaluator may also use a screen-recording tool and an audio recorder to record the words and actions of the user as the tasks are completed.

After the walkthrough is complete, the evaluator should look through the recordings for any problems, gaps, or ideas for the design of the task or activity under evaluation (Spencer, 2000). The evaluator should take notes on what worked, what did not work, what was confusing, and what was easy. For example, the learner completing the cognitive walkthrough may ask the evaluator, "Why would I use this feature of the social media to do this?" or "Why am I using a collaboration tool to do this task?"

This type of evaluation is useful when integrating social media or collaboration tools because focus can be placed on learners' use of the software in order to complete a larger activity. This will allow the evaluator to identify any technical issues with the tool. It will also help identify any misalignment between the tool and the activity before the activity is introduced to a broader audience. The evaluator can recommend changes or additions to the activity based on this information.

CONDUCTING A PILOT STUDY

While it is tempting to jump into the implementation phase of an activity that integrates a new social media or collaboration tool, it is best to take it slow. The cognitive walkthrough described previously is a good entrance into a pilot study because it helps to look at the specific details of the activity and how individual users interact with the tool. A pilot study takes this up a notch.

A pilot study is like a dress rehearsal. All of the components of the activity should be ready and working. All instructions, tools, prompts, resources, and guides should be complete and available to the appropriate stakeholders. The learning activity should take place in the learners' typical environment and at the typical time and day.

However, only a small group of people will be in the "audience." This is the difference between a pilot study and a full implementation. A pilot study is an insurance plan in case something unexpected goes wrong when a full group of individuals are completing an activity at the same time. Some important points to take into account when setting up a pilot study are:

- What are the goals of the pilot study?
- How will we know if the pilot study is successful or not?
- What do we expect to happen (hypothesis)?
- What will we do after the pilot if it is successful?
- What will we do after the pilot if it is not successful?
- Who will lead the pilot study and who will support that person?
- What will take place during the pilot? (specific steps or checkpoints)
- Who will be part of the pilot group?
- Who will notify the individuals who are part of the pilot group?
- What will we tell those who are not in the pilot group?
- What will those who are not in the pilot group do during the pilot?
- When will the pilot take place?
- How long will the pilot last?
- What will the pilot participants need (resources, tools, materials, content)?
- How will we provide the participants with what they need?
- What sort of data will we collect during the pilot? (observations, reactions, surveys)
- How will these data help us reach our goals?
- Who will analyze this data?

These points are just a snapshot of questions to ask during a pilot. Every pilot study is unique and may require more planning, expertise, or resources. There are many resources available that discuss how to conduct a good pilot study.

When integrating a new social media tool or collaboration tool as part of a broader learning experience, it is critical to conduct a pilot study. There may be technical, conceptual, or procedural issues that were not expected and need to be resolved before rolling out to a larger audience. The pilot study is a form of formative evaluation that will help make the overall learning experience more robust and successful in the end.

STEPPING BACK AND MOVING FORWARD

The evaluation methods described above are nowhere near exhaustive. Rather, they are just three examples that are commonly used in learning design and development today.

No matter the method used, it is critical to intentionally step back to evaluate the opinions, tools, activities, processes, and experiences relative to learning, teaching, or training. Evaluations should occur before, during, and after the activity or tool is implemented. It is important to evaluate early and often.

Over time, more and more social media and collaboration tools and activities will be designed or redesigned for specific learning experiences. With this iterative process, some activities and tools will be failures and some will be successes. Amid all of these, there will be increments of innovation and change.

Social media and collaboration tools will look very different in the future. Three-dimensional holograms and virtual reality simulations are two examples of technologies on the horizon that may change the way we socialize and collaborate with each other. Determining whether and how these will be valuable in the classroom will require extensive planning, testing, and evaluating.

Innovation and change are often the result of looking outside of the box when thinking about everyday practices and problems. They come about by solving problems with new or unlikely approaches. What is a problem today may become the source of a new social or collaboration tool tomorrow.

DISCUSSION AND EXERCISES

1. It is important to gauge learners' perspectives when designing a learning activity rather than making assumptions that may be false and lead to bad

design. Create a ten-question survey to determine what learners think about a specific social media or collaboration tool as part of a learning activity. Make sure to ask questions about:

(a) level of familiarity with the tool, etc.
(b) typical use of the tool
(c) their beliefs or opinions about the tool as part of the learning experience

Conduct the survey and provide a summary of the learners' responses as well as recommendations for improvement of the learning experience based on their responses.

2. Conduct a cognitive walkthrough of a learning activity that uses a social media or collaboration tool. This will require you to identify and communicate to your users four to five tasks to complete using the tool. For instance, five tasks for a cognitive walkthrough of a Skype group call might be: login, create an account, add contacts, create a Skype group call, and share a link. Ask each user to complete each task one at a time while you record their actions (on-screen and in-person) and your responses to these two questions:

"1. Will the user know what to do at this step?" and "2. If the user does the right thing, will they know that they did the right thing, and are making progress towards their goal?" (Spencer, 2000, p. 355)

Be sure to ask your users to say "Start" and "Done" for each task. After all the tasks are complete, you can stop and interview the user about their experience completing the tasks (general opinions, what was confusing, what they would change, etc.). Based on the cognitive walkthrough and the user feedback, write a brief report on:

(a) the strength of the social media or collaboration tool in helping users meet learning goals
(b) opportunities for improvement
(c) your recommendations for improvement

3. Draft a plan for piloting a new learning activity that integrates social media or collaboration tools in your organization. Use the questions listed in this chapter to help you decide who will participate, what the pilot will involve, where the pilot will take place, when the pilot will take place, why you are creating and piloting this new learning activity, and how the pilot will help you evaluate the learning activity.

REFERENCES

Intel Corporation. (n.d.). 50 years of Moore's Law. Retrieved March 30, 2018, from https://www.intel.com/content/www/us/en/silicon-innovations/moores-law-technology.html

Spencer, R. (2000, April). The streamlined cognitive walkthrough method, working around social constraints encountered in a software development company. In *Proceedings of the SIGCHI Conference on Human Factors in Computing Systems* (pp. 353–359). ACM.

Appendix A

Common Social Media and Technology Resources

American Educational Research Association (AERA)
http://www.aera.net/
American Technology Education Association
http://ateaonline.org
ASCD (Association for Supervision and Curriculum Development)
http://www.ascd.org
Association for Educational Communications and Technology (AECT)
https://www.aect.org/
Association for Talent Development
https://www.td.org
Center for Technology in Learning
http://www.sri.com/about/organization/education/ctl
Consortium for School Networking (CoSN)
http://www.cosn.org/
Educause
http://www.educause.edu
International Society for Technology in Education
http://www.iste.org
MacArthur Foundation: Digital Media and Learning
http://www.macfound.org/programs/learning/
National Center for Educational Statistics (NCES)
http://nces.ed.gov
Online Learning Consortium (OLC), formerly the Sloan Consortium
http://onlinelearningconsortium.org/
Social Media Association http://socialmediaassoc.com/

U.S. Department of Education Protecting Student Privacy
https://studentprivacy.ed.gov/
U.S. Department of Education Office of Educational Technology
http://tech.ed.gov/

Appendix B

Social Media and Technology Trademarks

The following trademarks are listed in alphabetical order.

Android, Google, Google Drive, Google Docs, Presentation, YouTube, Hangouts, Chrome, Chromebook, Chromecast, Googlecast, and Drive are trademarks of Google, Inc.
Apple, iPhone, iPad, iPad Air, Mac, Macintosh, MacBook Pro, OSX, AppleTV, Apple II, MacOS X, Keynote, Pages, Numbers are registered trademarks of Apple, Inc.
Edmodo is a registered trademark of Edmodo, Inc.
Facebook is a registered trademark of Facebook, Inc.
GoToMeeting is a registered trademark of LogMeIn, Inc.
IBM and IBM PC are registered trademarks of International Business Machines, Inc.
Instagram is a trademark of Facebook, Inc.
iOS is a registered trademark of Cisco and used under license by Apple, Inc.
LinkedIn is a registered trademark of LinkedIn Corporation.
Microsoft, Microsoft Office, PowerPoint, Word, Outlook, Excel, Microsoft Windows, Microsoft Sharepoint, and Windows 10 are registered trademarks of Microsoft Corp.
Pinterest is a registered trademark of Pinterest, Inc.
RealTimeBoard is a registered trademark of RealTimeBoard, Inc.
Skype is a trademark of Skype Limited.
Slack is a registered trademark of Slack Technologies, Inc.
Snapchat is a registered trademark of Snap, Inc.
Trello is a registered trademark of Trello, Inc.

Twitter is a registered trademark of Twitter, Inc.
Wi-Fi is a registered trademark of the Wi-Fi Alliance.
Wikipedia and Wikimedia are registered trademarks of the Wikimedia Foundation.
Zoom is a registered trademark of Zoom Video Communications, Inc.

Appendix C

Create Accessible Video and Social Media

A compilation of federal guidance, checklists, and testing information for creating and maintaining accessible video, multimedia, and social media using various popular electronic formats and channels including Twitter, Facebook, YouTube, Vine, Wordpress, and other social media tools. Sources for these resources are identified by abbreviations for federal components.

Other valuable guidance from nonfederal sources, including industry and academia, can be found from Internet search using relevant keywords such as "accessible presentation." Guidance: methods, tips, and techniques on how to author and check social media: Section 508 accessibility.

Social media

- Making Twitter Images Accessible: innovative technique from the 18F group at GSA.
- Social Media and Accessibility: Resources to Know, January 2015: informative post on digitalgov with links to other resources.
- Federal Social Media Accessibility Toolkit, June 2014: comprehensive guide to Improving the Accessibility of Social Media in Government developed by DOL, GSA, and the Federal Social Media Community of Practice, originally a digitalgov post now available as a collaborative "HackPad" for others to contribute.
- Accessing Social Media, July 2014: proceedings from a cross-sector event about making social media tools and content accessible including information about authoring tools, client apps, and best practices from FCC.
- Five (5) Myths About Social Media Accessibility, June 2013: post on digitalgov.

- Making Social Media More Accessible (link is external), December 2012: specific tips for making your agency's social media content more accessible from DigitalGov University by GSA. [video]

Video and multimedia

Guidance: methods, tips, and techniques on how to author and check video and multimedia presentations to make them Section 508 accessible.

- Creating Accessible Flash Course, April 2014: online tutorial from VA.
- 508 Accessible Videos—How to Make Audio Descriptions, June 2014: post on digitalgov with practical guidance from GSA.
- 508 Accessible Videos—How to Caption Videos, June 2014: post on digitalgov with practical guidance from GSA.
- 508 Accessible Videos—Use a 508-Compliant Video Player, June 2014: post on digitalgov.
- 508 Accessible Videos—Why (and How) to Make Them, June 2014: post on digitalgov with comprehensive guidance.
- Provisional Guidance for Audio Description (AD), September 2014: draft guidance on audio description from HHS.
- Alternate Text for Images, July 2011: key concepts, guidance, and SSA common mistakes.

Source: United States General Services Administration, Section508.gov

Appendix D

Electronic Code of Federal Regulations

Part 312 Children's Online Privacy Protection Rule

§312.3 Regulation of unfair or deceptive acts or practices in connection with the collection, use, and/or disclosure of personal information from and about children on the Internet.

General requirements. It shall be unlawful for any operator of a website or online service directed to children, or any operator that has actual knowledge that it is collecting or maintaining personal information from a child, to collect personal information from a child in a manner that violates the regulations prescribed under this part. Generally, under this part, an operator must:

(a) Provide notice on the website or online service of what information it collects from children, how it uses such information, and its disclosure practices for such information (§312.4(b));
(b) Obtain verifiable parental consent prior to any collection, use, and/or disclosure of personal information from children (§312.5);
(c) Provide a reasonable means for a parent to review the personal information collected from a child and to refuse to permit its further use or maintenance (§312.6);
(d) Not condition a child's participation in a game, the offering of a prize, or another activity on the child disclosing more personal information than is reasonably necessary to participate in such activity (§312.7); and
(e) Establish and maintain reasonable procedures to protect the confidentiality, security, and integrity of personal information collected from children (§312.8).

Source: Electronic Code of Federal Regulations (e-CFR)

Appendix E

ELCC Building and District Level Standards

ELCC Standard 1.0: A building-level education leader applies knowledge that promotes the success of every student by collaboratively facilitating the development, articulation, implementation, and stewardship of a shared school vision of learning through the collection and use of data to identify school goals, assess organizational effectiveness, and implement school plans to achieve school goals; promotion of continual and sustainable school improvement; and evaluation of school progress and revision of school plans supported by school-based stakeholders.

1.1: Candidates understand and can collaboratively develop, articulate, implement, and steward a shared vision of learning for a school.
1.2: Candidates understand and can collect and use data to identify school goals, assess organizational effectiveness, and implement plans to achieve school goals.
1.3: Candidates understand and can promote continual and sustainable school improvement.
1.4: Candidates understand and can evaluate school progress and revise school plans supported by school stakeholders.

ELCC Standard 1.0: A district-level education leader applies knowledge that promotes the success of every student by facilitating the development, articulation, implementation, and stewardship of a shared district vision of learning through the collection and use of data to identify district goals, assess organizational effectiveness, and implement district plans to achieve district goals; promotion of continual and sustainable district improvement;

and evaluation of district progress and revision of district plans supported by district stakeholders.

1.1: Candidates understand and can collaboratively develop, articulate, implement, and steward a shared district vision of learning for a school district.
1.2: Candidates understand and can collect and use data to identify district goals, assess organizational effectiveness, and implement district plans to achieve district goals.
1.3: Candidates understand and can promote continual and sustainable district improvement.
1.4: Candidates understand and can evaluate district progress and revise district plans supported by district stakeholders.

ELCC Standard 2.0: A building-level education leader applies knowledge that promotes the success of every student by sustaining a school culture and instructional program conducive to student learning through collaboration, trust, and a personalized learning environment with high expectations for students; creating and evaluating a comprehensive, rigorous and coherent curricular and instructional school program; developing and supervising the instructional and leadership capacity of school staff; and promoting the most effective and appropriate technologies to support teaching and learning within a school environment.

2.1: Candidates understand and can sustain a school culture and instructional program conducive to student learning through collaboration, trust, and a personalized learning environment with high expectations for students.
2.2: Candidates understand and can create and evaluate a comprehensive, rigorous, and coherent curricular and instructional school program.
2.3: Candidates understand and can develop and supervise the instructional and leadership capacity of school staff.
2.4: Candidates understand and can promote the most effective and appropriate technologies to support teaching and learning in a school environment.

ELCC Standard 2.0: A district-level education leader applies knowledge that promotes the success of every student by sustaining a district culture conducive to collaboration, trust, and a personalized learning environment with high expectations for students; creating and evaluating a comprehensive, rigorous, and coherent curricular and instructional district program; developing and supervising the instructional and leadership capacity across the district; and promoting the most effective and appropriate technologies to support teaching and learning within the district.

2.1: Candidates understand and can advocate, nurture, and sustain a district culture and instructional program conducive to student learning through collaboration, trust, and a personalized learning environment with high expectations for students.
2.2: Candidates understand and can create and evaluate a comprehensive, rigorous, and coherent curricular and instructional district program.
2.3: Candidates understand and can develop and supervise the instructional and leadership capacity across the district.
2.4: Candidates understand and can promote the most effective and appropriate district technologies to support teaching and learning within the district.

ELCC Standard 3.0: A building-level education leader applies knowledge that promotes the success of every student by ensuring the management of the school organization, operation, and resources through monitoring and evaluating the school management and operational systems; efficiently using human, fiscal, and technological resources in a school environment; promoting and protecting the welfare and safety of school students and staff; developing school capacity for distributed leadership; and ensuring that teacher and organizational time is focused to support high-quality instruction and student learning.

3.1: Candidates understand and can monitor and evaluate school management and operational systems.
3.2: Candidates understand and can efficiently use human, fiscal, and technological resources to manage school operations.
3.3: Candidates understand and can promote school-based policies and procedures that protect the welfare and safety of students and staff within the school.
3.4: Candidates understand and can develop school capacity for distributed leadership.

3.5: Candidates understand and can ensure teacher and organizational time focuses on supporting high-quality school instruction and student learning.

ELCC Standard 3.0: A district-level education leader applies knowledge that promotes the success of every student by ensuring the management of the district's organization, operation, and resources through monitoring and evaluating district management and operational systems; efficiently using human, fiscal, and technological resources within the district; promoting district-level policies and procedures that protect the welfare and safety of students and staff across the district; developing district capacity for distributed leadership; and ensuring that district time focuses on high-quality instruction and student learning.

3.1: Candidates understand and can monitor and evaluate district management and operational systems.
3.2: Candidates understand and can efficiently use human, fiscal, and technological resources within the district.
3.3: Candidates understand and can promote district-level policies and procedures that protect the welfare and safety of students and staff across the district.
3.4: Candidates understand and can develop district capacity for distributed leadership.
3.5: Candidates understand and can ensure that district time focuses on supporting high-quality school instruction and student learning.

ELCC Standard 4.0: A building-level education leader applies knowledge that promotes the success of every student by collaborating with faculty and community members, responding to diverse community interests and needs, and mobilizing community resources on behalf of the school by collecting and analyzing information pertinent to improvement of the school's educational environment; promoting an understanding, appreciation, and use of the diverse cultural, social, and intellectual resources within the school community; building and sustaining positive school relationships with families and caregivers; and cultivating productive school relationships with community partners.

4.1: Candidates understand and can collaborate with faculty and community members by collecting and analyzing information pertinent to the improvement of the school's educational environment.

4.2: Candidates understand and can mobilize community resources by promoting an understanding, appreciation, and use of diverse cultural, social, and intellectual resources within the school community.
4.3: Candidates understand and can respond to community interests and needs by building and sustaining positive school relationships with families and caregivers.
4.4: Candidates understand and can respond to community interests and needs by building and sustaining productive school relationships with community partners.

ELCC Standard 4.0: A district-level education leader applies knowledge that promotes the success of every student by collaborating with faculty and community members, responding to diverse community interests and needs, and mobilizing community resources for the district by collecting and analyzing information pertinent to improvement of the district's educational environment; promoting an understanding, appreciation, and use of the community's diverse cultural, social, and intellectual resources throughout the district; building and sustaining positive district relationships with families and caregivers; and cultivating productive district relationships with community partners.

4.1: Candidates understand and can collaborate with faculty and community members by collecting and analyzing information pertinent to the improvement of the district's educational environment.
4.2: Candidates understand and can mobilize community resources by promoting understanding, appreciation, and use of the community's diverse cultural, social, and intellectual resources throughout the district.
4.3: Candidates understand and can respond to community interests and needs by building and sustaining positive district relationships with families and caregivers.
4.4: Candidates understand and can respond to community interests and needs by building and sustaining productive district relationships with community partners.

ELCC Standard 5.0: A building-level education leader applies knowledge that promotes the success of every student by acting with integrity, fairness, and in an ethical manner to ensure a school system of accountability for every student's academic and social success by modeling school principles of self-awareness, reflective practice, transparency, and ethical behavior as related to their roles within the school; safeguarding the values of democracy, equity, and diversity within the school; evaluating the potential moral and legal consequences of decision making in the school; and promoting social justice within the school to ensure that individual student needs inform all aspects of schooling.

5.1: Candidates understand and can act with integrity and fairness to ensure a school system of accountability for every student's academic and social success.
5.2: Candidates understand and can model principles of self-awareness, reflective practice, transparency, and ethical behavior as related to their roles within the school.
5.3: Candidates understand and can safeguard the values of democracy, equity, and diversity within the school.
5.4: Candidates understand and can evaluate the potential moral and legal consequences of decision-making in the school.
5.5: Candidates understand and can promote social justice within the school to ensure that individual student needs inform all aspects of schooling.

ELCC Standard 5.0: A district-level education leader applies knowledge that promotes the success of every student by acting with integrity, fairness, and in an ethical manner to ensure a district system of accountability for every student's academic and social success by modeling district principles of self-awareness, reflective practice, transparency, and ethical behavior as related to their roles within the district; safeguarding the values of democracy, equity, and diversity within the district; evaluating the potential moral and legal consequences of decision making in the district; and promoting social justice within the district to ensure individual student needs inform all aspects of schooling.

5.1: Candidates understand and can act with integrity and fairness to ensure a district system of accountability for every student's academic and social success.
5.2: Candidates understand and can model principles of self-awareness, reflective practice, transparency, and ethical behavior as related to their roles within the district.
5.3: Candidates understand and can safeguard the values of democracy, equity, and diversity within the district.
5.4: Candidates understand and can evaluate the potential moral and legal consequences of decision-making in the district.
5.5: Candidates understand and can promote social justice within the district to ensure individual student needs inform all aspects of schooling.

ELCC Standard 6.0: A building-level education leader applies knowledge that promotes the success of every student by understanding, responding to, and influencing the larger political, social, economic, legal, and cultural context through advocating for school students, families, and caregivers; acting to influence local, district, state, and national decisions affecting student learning in a school environment; and anticipating and assessing emerging trends and initiatives in order to adapt school-based leadership strategies.

- 6.1: Candidates understand and can advocate for school students, families, and caregivers.
- 6.2: Candidates understand and can act to influence local, district, state, and national decisions affecting student learning in a school environment.
- 6.3: Candidates understand and can anticipate and assess emerging trends and initiatives in order to adapt school-based leadership strategies.

ELCC Standard 6.0: A district-level education leader applies knowledge that promotes the success of every student by understanding, responding to, and influencing the larger political, social, economic, legal, and cultural context within the district through advocating for district students, families, and caregivers; acting to influence local, district, state, and national decisions affecting student learning; and anticipating and assessing emerging trends and initiatives in order to adapt district-level leadership strategies.

- 6.1: Candidates understand and can advocate for district students, families, and caregivers.
- 6.2: Candidates understand and can act to influence local, district, state, and national decisions affecting student learning in a district environment.
- 6.3: Candidates understand and can anticipate and assess emerging trends and initiatives in order to adapt district-level leadership strategies.

ELCC Standard 7.0: A building-level education leader applies knowledge that promotes the success of every student through a substantial and sustained educational leadership internship experience that has school-based field experiences and clinical internship practice within a school setting and is monitored by a qualified, on-site mentor.

- 7.1: Substantial Field and Clinical Internship Experience: The program provides significant field experiences and clinical internship practice for candidates within a school environment to synthesize and apply the content knowledge and develop professional skills identified in the other *Educational Leadership Building-Level Program Standards* through authentic, school-based leadership experiences.

7.2: Sustained Internship Experience: Candidates are provided a six-month, concentrated (nine to twelve hours per week) internship that includes field experiences within a school-based environment.

7.3: Qualified On-Site Mentor: An on-site school mentor who has demonstrated experience as an educational leader within a school and is selected collaboratively by the intern and program faculty with training by the supervising institution.

ELCC Standard 7.0: A district-level education leader applies knowledge that promotes the success of every student in a substantial and sustained educational leadership internship experience that has district-based field experiences and clinical practice within a district setting and is monitored by a qualified, on-site mentor.

7.1: Substantial Experience: The program provides significant field experiences and clinical internship practice for candidates within a district environment to synthesize and apply the content knowledge and develop professional skills identified in the other *Educational Leadership District-Level Program Standards* through authentic, district-based leadership experiences.

7.2: Sustained Experience: Candidates are provided a six-month concentrated (nine to twelve hours per week) internship that includes field experiences within a district environment.

7.3: Qualified On-site Mentor: An on-site district mentor who has demonstrated successful experience as an educational leader at the district level and is selected collaboratively by the intern and program faculty with training by the supervising institution.

Source: ELCC Standards, November 2011, National Policy Board For Educational Administration (NPBEA), The National Council for Accreditation of Teacher Education (NCATE) now Council for the Accreditation of Educator Preparation (CAEP).

Appendix F

Technology Standards for School Administrators

TSSA Framework, Standards, and Performance Indicators (v4.0)

I. Leadership and Vision—Educational leaders inspire a shared vision for comprehensive integration of technology and foster an environment and culture conducive to the realization of that vision.

Educational leaders:

A. facilitate the shared development by all stakeholders of a vision for technology use and widely communicate that vision.
B. maintain an inclusive and cohesive process to develop, implement, and monitor a dynamic, long-range, and systemic technology plan to achieve the vision.
C. foster and nurture a culture of responsible risk-taking and advocate policies promoting continuous innovation with technology.
D. use data in making leadership decisions.
E. advocate for research-based effective practices in the use of technology.
F. advocate on the state and national levels for policies, programs, and funding opportunities that support implementation of the district technology plan.

II. Learning and Teaching—Educational leaders ensure that curricular design, instructional strategies, and learning environments integrate appropriate technologies to maximize learning and teaching.

Educational leaders:

A. identify, use, evaluate, and promote appropriate technologies to enhance and support instruction and standards-based curriculum leading to high levels of student achievement.

B. facilitate and support collaborative technology-enriched learning environments conducive to innovation for improved learning.
C. provide for learner-centered environments that use technology to meet the individual and diverse needs of learners.
D. facilitate the use of technologies to support and enhance instructional methods that develop higher-level thinking, decision making, and problem-solving skills.
E. provide for and ensure that faculty and staff take advantage of quality professional learning opportunities for improved learning and teaching with technology.

III. Productivity and Professional Practice—Educational leaders apply technology to enhance their professional practice and increase their own productivity and of others.

Educational leaders:

A. model the routine, intentional, and effective use of technology.
B. employ technology for communication and collaboration among colleagues, staff, parents, students, and the larger community.
C. create and participate in learning communities that stimulate, nurture, and support faculty and staff in using technology for improved productivity.
D. engage in sustained, job-related professional learning using technology resources.
E. maintain awareness of emerging technologies and their potential uses in education.
F. use technology to advance organizational improvement.

IV. Support, Management, and Operations—Educational leaders ensure the integration of technology to support productive systems for learning and administration.

Educational leaders:

A. develop, implement, and monitor policies and guidelines to ensure compatibility of technologies.
B. implement and use integrated technology–based management and operations systems.
C. allocate financial and human resources to ensure complete and sustained implementation of the technology plan.
D. integrate strategic plans, technology plans, and other improvement plans and policies to align efforts and leverage resources.

E. implement procedures to drive continuous improvement of technology systems and to support technology replacement cycles.

V. Assessment and Evaluation—Educational leaders use technology to plan and implement comprehensive systems of effective assessment and evaluation.

Educational leaders:

A. use multiple methods to assess and evaluate appropriate uses of technology resources for learning, communication, and productivity.
B. use technology to collect and analyze data, interpret results, and communicate findings to improve instructional practice and student learning.
C. assess staff knowledge, skills, and performance in using technology and use results to facilitate quality professional development and to inform personnel decisions.
D. use technology to assess, evaluate, and manage administrative and operational systems.

VI. Social, Legal, and Ethical Issues—Educational leaders understand the social, legal, and ethical issues related to technology and model responsible decision making related to these issues.

Educational leaders:

A. ensure equity of access to technology resources that enable and empower all learners and educators.
B. identify, communicate, model, and enforce social, legal, and ethical practices to promote responsible use of technology.
C. promote and enforce privacy, security, and online safety related to the use of technology.
D. promote and enforce environmentally safe and healthy practices in the use of technology.
E. participate in the development of policies that clearly enforce copyright law and assign ownership of intellectual property developed with district resources.

Source: These standards are the property of the TSSA Collaborative and may not be altered without written permission. The following notice must accompany reproduction of these standards: "This material was originally produced as a project of the Technology Standards for School Administrators Collaborative." Foundation Standards Developed by the TSSA Collaborative Draft v4.0 4 Draft Date 11/5/01

Index

achievement, 1, 48, 49
advertising, 37, 44, 82
Age Discrimination in Employment Act (ADEA), 82, 85
amendments, 82–83, 90–91
American Disabilities Act (ADA), 82, 85
artifacts, 25–27, 60–66
assessment, 11–17, 94, 124

behaviors, 11, 14, 48, 49, 88, 94, 118–19
blogging, 77, 80
Bloom's taxonomy, 14–15
brainstorming, 64, 66
bullying, 37, 41, 89–90

cease and desist, 79
chat, 19, 38–41, 57–59, 64–67
Civil Right Act, 1964, 80–84
cloud, 5, 35, 57
cognitive apprenticeship, 22, 27–30
collaboration, 56–70
collaboration tool, 56–70
common law, 78
communication, 8–9, 39, 41, 56–57
connectivism, 31–32
constructionism, 24–27
contests, 49

defamation, 76–78, 88–89
delegating, 67
digital age, 5
discrimination, 81–85
domains of learning, 15
drafting, 67

Edmodo, 37
email, 39
employment laws, 80
Equal Employment Opportunity Commission (EEOC), 80
Equal Pay Act, 82

Facebook, 36
face-to-face, 41, 68, 89
fair use, 79
Federal Communication Commission, 79
free stuff, 50

Google, 58–59
GoToMeeting, 59
group contacts, 40

hand raising, 65
harassment, 76, 82, 84
Hatch Act, 77

identity construction environment, 25
individual contacts, 39
information sharing, 68
Instructional Software Design Project, 25
instructionism, 23
instruments for assessment, 16
integrative learning, 25
intuitive technology, 60–62

learning activities, 10, 33, 66, 103
learning objectives, 13–17
legal issues, 75–91
legitimate peripheral participation, 27–28
level of performance, 14, 28
LinkedIn, 36, 37, 40

meeting recording, 65
monitoring interactions, 44

National Security Agency, 79

peer review, 67
planning, 11–12
polling, 65
portfolios, 16, 49
presentation mode, 65
privacy settings, 44
project-based learning, 25–26
public domain, 79

reactions, 41
real-time editing, 65

scaffolding, 23, 26–27
screen sharing, 65
Skype, 57–58
Slack, 61–62
Snapchat, 36
social media: association, 79, 91; laws, 89; tools, 36–51
sociotechnical system, 25
stalking, 45, 89, 91
student legal issues, 88

team games, 67
text message, 39
themed content pages, 43, 48
threats of violence, 90
Twitter, 36, 46

United States Bill of Rights, 75, 77

video call, 58, 64
virtual reality, 6, 32, 104
voice call, 57, 64

whiteboard, 60, 65
Wikipedia, 61

YouTube, 36

zone of proximal development, 23, 48
Zoom, 59

About the Authors

Kathryn Wozniak is assistant professor of instructional design and technology at Concordia University Chicago. She is passionate about the design of digital learning experiences and environments for learners of all ages. She has published and presented on topics including learning technologies, social learning, metacognition, gamification, and competence-based learning. In addition to her experience in higher education, Dr. Wozniak has extensive experience working with corporate and nonprofit clients. She teaches courses on human–computer interaction, multimedia design, and computer-supported collaborative learning.

Daniel R. Tomal is distinguished professor of leadership at Concordia University Chicago. He has published over twenty books (several with RLE) and over 200 article studies and articles. He has testified before the United States Congress, has consulted for numerous schools and organizations, and teaches and consults in leadership and technology areas. He is a former school administrator, high school teacher, and corporate vice president. He has made guest appearances on many national and local television and radio shows such as CBS *This Morning*, NBC *Cover to Cover*, ABC, *Les Brown*, *Joan Rivers*, *Chicago Talks*.

www.ingramcontent.com/pod-product-compliance
Lightning Source LLC
Chambersburg PA
CBHW021852300426
44115CB00005B/124